THIS IS ME

The Life and Writings
of a Young Poet
1987 – 2006

BY ALEX WARE
with reflections by family and friends

STELLAR
COMMUNICATIONS
HOUSTON

Paperback ISBN: 978-1-944952-07-5

Stellar Communications Houston
www.stellarwriter.com
281.804.7089

Written by Alex Ware with reflections by family and friends
Editing by Mark Dostert of Writespace Houston
Developmental editing and preparation for publication by Ella Hearrean Ritchie
Cover design and formatting by Jamie Tipton
Cover drawing by Alex Ware
Cover photo by Corrina Pariyar

For Alex

His nineteen years were filled with love,
laughter, confusion, fear, and
always with a sense of never-ending hope
by those who loved him that each year of life
would bring him closer to the peace he desired.

And for Jason

You were the best wedding gift
I received when I married Richard.
You have grown into an honorable man
who puts your family's needs before yours
and who has endured the same loss
of a son as I have.

THE BOOK

I wish I was

A book so

You would have

Words when you

Try to read me.

I wish I was

Jesus

So you'd understand

That people need

Me.

I wish I was almost enough

Instead of being

Almost nothing

And see who

I really am.

– Alex, 2002

CONTENTS

Pat with Alex at Mount Bachelor, Oregon, 2004.

FOREWORD

MOTHER

Remember me when I am free
of all that was
wasn't
and couldn't be

– by Alex, 2002

It has been more than ten years since my son, Alex, left this world. He took his life when he was nineteen years old. Alex was a writer, poet, and artist as well as a treasured son, brother, nephew, uncle, stepson, and friend. He was a mysterious, complicated, and much-loved boy and young man.

This Is Me is a celebration of his thirtieth birthday. It is a compilation of some of his poetry and writing, school assignments, notes, and drawings along with reflections by some of the people he left behind. The material covers from age seven to the night he died. During that twelve-year span of time, Alex produced a volume of work that is unusual, both in quantity and in the topics covered.

The material has been compiled with much help, and the pieces are arranged as thoughtfully as possible to reflect the time period in which Alex was writing. Some spelling and grammatical mistakes have been left unedited because they are either age-appropriate or are presented in his own handwriting. Some are stylistic choices made by Alex.

As you read through Alex's writings and see his drawings, you will see his humor, quirky use of words, prophetic thoughts, and pain. Friends and family will recognize the names and places that are mentioned in some of his writings. If you didn't know Alex, you will meet a free spirit, a deep thinker, and a lover of animals, always seeking answers to life's mysterious ways with his quick wit and sharp intellect.

Welcome to his inner world.

Pat Stone

SELECTIONS
from 1994-1997

≈≡≈

7 – 10 YEARS OLD
Mountain View Elementary, Waco, Texas

Alex with his mom and dad at a Thanksgiving
celebration at Lake Shore Baptist Children's Center,
Waco, Texas.

REFLECTIONS

Alex always threw up his hand in response to the
question, "Who wants to go to Toys 'R' Us?"

BY LIBBY LANGFORD

Alex's best childhood friend in Waco, Texas

Best friends Libby and Alex with Alex's dog, Yellow.

I was an only child, but I didn't always feel like one after the day I met my next door neighbor. I was five years old, and he was three when we met at the end of our driveways on Sugg Drive. From that day forward we would spend every moment our parents allowed together. I don't know if he was more of a brother or a soul mate (not romantically), but he taught me how to love unconditionally.

I have so many fond memories; they are like the puzzle pieces that create my childhood. If he was home he would greet me as soon as I pulled up in the driveway from school or one of my sport's practices. Some of our favorite things were playing on my swing set pretending that there was hot lava or sharks below, climbing the amazing tree in his front yard, building some amazing forts, riding our bicycles to Baskin Robbins, playing spies or going to the Family Y to swim all summer long. We jumped on his trampoline, made potions out of the neighbor's flowers, and played in the creek behind his dad's house.

I remember our play names were Mikey and Michelle, but I don't recall why. I remember our trips to Six Flags and snowboarding in Colorado, and going out to our favorite pizza places Poppa Rollo's and GattiLand. I remember his birthday parties at the Discovery Center, his dad taking us to Toys-R-Us for a new action figure for each of us, his mom's Volvo, their three-legged dog, his dad's little convertible, going to Kiddie Land and how his mom made the best Kraft Mac-N-Cheese. These are just some of my favorite memories but there is an entire childhood full. He was my childhood, my world.

Even when he moved to Hereford for a few of my middle school years, we still messaged back and forth on the computer and talked on the phone. When he came back for high school, I was elated. He was there when I started getting interested in boys, learned how to drive, and discovered electronic music and raves. I still have never met a guy that could move like him and dance so well. We only had two fights that were significant enough to even remember; the first one was when he borrowed my Splinter action figure and returned it with the head missing, and the other was when we were teenagers and were doing things we shouldn't have been doing in the first place.

He had so many strengths and gave me strength when I needed it most. He was the most kind, compassionate, open-minded person and believed that everyone deserved a chance in this world. He didn't define people by color, sexual preference, income, religion or age. Instead, he embraced diversity and uniqueness.

I have kept all of his letters, pictures, and art. But what I cherish most is all our memories. I am the luckiest person in the world to be able to grow up with him. He impacted me more than any one person has my whole entire life.

His impact was so profound that I in fact named my only child after him – Alexandria "Alex" Lyla. I wish we could grow old together. We even discussed getting married and having kids if we didn't find anyone else. Pat and Nathan have gotten the chance to get to know and love my daughter Alex, and I cannot imagine how amazing he would be with her.

I have already started to share just a few pictures and stories with my daughter about who I named her after. I will show her the Peace Garden and his tree and will take her to the Discovery Center one day. She has already played with his favorite stuffed animal named Growly the Polar Bear!

The love he showed me and the love I have for him cannot be put into words and is infinite. I have never felt pain like the pain I felt when I lost you and have prayed to see you in my dreams ever since. I now know that part of you is still with me. Knowing and loving you are what made me who I am today.

I miss you; I love you, my friend, my brother, my soul. Memories of you will be with me always, but also know that a puzzle piece from my adult life will forever be missing.

Libby's daughter, Alex.

BY PENNY MALOY GIFFORD

A close friend of the family who was there when Alex arrived and when he died—and always close by for all the days in between.

Penny and Alex in Hereford, May 1997.

I'm not much of a writer, and my memory is sketchy, but here we go.

The first recollections of Alex are when he was "Ozer." His mom will have to remind me why we gave him that nickname in the womb. I also recall her despair when the ultrasound made the doctors think that his brain was damaged. She thought it was because of cleaning the litter box and toxoplasmosis. She ate so much fish after that for "brain food." Thank God that his brain was all there – and all that fish certainly did make him smart!

As a toddler he was definitely cute. Certainly Minnie thought so!!

It was nice to have the attic on Valley Mills for him to claim as his own. Maybe he did some writing up there.

Driving out to deliver Meals on Wheels once, he educated me about "Nine Inch Nails." I had never heard of the band, and he was happy to tell me about them. I asked him about the name, and he told me it had to do with the nails that were used to hang Jesus on the cross.

He liked showing his aunt Karen and me his park in Hereford when we came up for his mom's first brain event. He was either very proud of his park, or it was just a ploy to get us out of the house!

How old was he when he decided he was a Buddhist? That he was not going to eat meat? One determined young boy, young man. Loved him.

SCHOOL
ASSIGNMENTS

Alex studying at his desk
with a photo of his "Bubba" Jason.

Name: Alex

"No one else has a pet like mine!"
Tell me about your pet.

My dog has onle three
legis. It comes to my mam
I like her. evre morning. evre were
ny mom gos my dog gos to.
She nevr comes with me.
She is gray. She is vere
talinted. she likes to eat
cugcakes. Shel eat inethan
ant her ers hangdawn.
but I stil love her vare
vare mosh. she is my faveitis
dog in the hold wrld. she
skrashis me wen she.
whts to shak my hand.

Alex with Lucy, the three-legged
Weimaraner, and his favorite cat, Kelly.

my mom
my mom. is 24s. I love
her. she is my fravrest
mom in the hold
wrld! I like Libby
selsent best. Beau is my
thend best friend. my
mom is gritey no one
is pretexer then my
mom. I am riting
this becose tomaro is
mothers day. no one
else has a mom
like mine. if eney
botey ders to mess
with my mom I
will give them a
nukil ban winch.
no one messes with
my mom upslept
me I will fite for
my mom! do you
hear me out ther! I
frene if you lay
one frenger on
my mom you are
dead!§§ I sownt like a

reisier. so get your eyes on the wrds our if will boty salam you to if you nede rea look at this storey ant fell rite at nome if you don't like it report to me and I will re... the art that you dident like. so kep on reading the storey so I can ...ingoey the pese and aut out slide ant mabe read the ...es bapr. ant if you like the my storey tell me becaus I will be prad uv wat I rote Xskyoos me wat did I hear you did ent like it I nede to kill him!

POETRY, NOTES, & DRAWINGS

SUMMER VACATION

on my summer vacation I will go to
new York to see one of my moms friend
I thenk it wood be fun to go to my
moms friends house in new York. It
wood be fun to be in the sitty.

ALEX May 17, 1994

First,Get a cup and cleen it off.

Then,get some ice.

Then,get a mountindew.

Then,get a dr. peper.

Then,Then get the rest of the
softdrinkes Next,ster it up

Last,then you have a soeside drink.

by, Alex

From: PMGJJG@aol.om

To: natpat@wtrt.net

Subject: alal

Date: Monday, August 03, 1998 8:55 PM

hello mommy, it's me alex and i'm at penny's. i ate at Jason's deli. i ate a grilled cheese sandwich, potato chips, a pickle and two helpings of chocolate ice cream. penny, viki, bailey, tiffin and me. I miss you. Sincerely love best friend and son, alex warehouse, the duck # 3.

SELECTIONS
from 1997 − 2000

10 − 12 YEARS OLD
Shirley Elementary, Hereford, Texas
Redbud Academy, Amarillo, Texas

Alex in Hereford, Texas.

REFLECTIONS

Alex at Disney World, 1999.

BY LINDA BENGE JACKSON

A letter of recommendation the director of Redbud Academy to the director of Coe Academy, July 31, 2001.

Alex Ware attended Redbud Academy from the fall of 1999 until fall of 2000. Academically, Alex did quite well in subjects that were language based, particularly literature. He was not particularly enthusiastic about history, but his reading was exceptional, and advanced for his age. He also wrote poetry, which he sometimes shared with staff.

He was frustrated with algebra, but often did very well in geometry. Since the group of friends he associated with were interested in geography, he soon developed an interest in the area and achieved status by competing well in our geography bees.

He was creative, talkative, loved dancing and acting games, and often caused excitement among his friends. This was fun for them, but occasionally led to disciplining problems, because Alex liked to see how far he could push the limits. He often questioned rules, sometimes to the point of trying our patience.

Mostly though, we found him enjoyable, intelligent, and creative. He was above average in literature based subjects and reluctant in subjects he disliked, such as math and history. He showed intense loyalty to friends, and was highly charismatic in his group, often being the leader and inventor of games.

We missed him when he left, even though things were much more peaceful at times. When he returned to us for visits, he was greeted with enthusiasm. We want to see Alex succeed and live up to the potential we know is there.

BY ELIZABETH WHITE-OLSEN

Alex's friend and 7th grade creative writing teacher at Redbud Academy

What I see here is evidence of a mind fully, courageously awakened to the incredible freshness and the incredible difficulties of life. Alex's writing has the fresh, wide-open spirit of a child's vibrant heart, with the wisdom of an adult's perceptions. He is one of the most unique people I've ever met, of the tens of thousands I have met in my life.

This is why we more passionate and dreamy adults loved him. He could relate to us on a much higher level than any other kids could, both because of his astounding intelligence and astounding confidence, yet he still had the whole, unbroken, wild enthusiasm of a kid. So, spending time with him, when you were really "with him" and let him be himself, brought you seamlessly back into the world of childhood. Within himself he bridged childhood and adulthood in a wonderful way. I think it's likely he was an adult long before he was an adult and a kid long past the time most teens had stopped being kids. This is one of the trillion things that was special about him.

Then, there was his style, which is incredibly evident in these pages. He had a natural predilection for the quirky. His style is quite evident through his surprising word choices, as well as through his use of unexpected rhyme and repetition. I found reading his work really moving, even when he wrote about his pain.

I think the conventional view on suicide is to say that the person who took his own life "failed" at something—"failed to live." "Failed to grow up." But, I bet Alex doesn't feel like he failed at anything. He ALWAYS stood by himself and stood by his own decisions. His strength was amazing and I can't help but imagine him also standing strong after his life.

Looking back, I think that if there was any "failure" in Alex's passing, it wasn't Alex's "failure" but rather, our vastly broken world that failed to give his soul a home. One view: Alex shined so bright and true, the world couldn't support him. Its wattage wasn't enough to support his great soul's needs.

Our world was a better world with Alex Ware squeezing its air in and out of his lungs, seeing and speaking loud and clearly about its charms and deficiencies, laughing and cutting up and innocently, nonchalantly freaking out every single person in a room.

You never had to explain things to Alex, and you could never explain to someone who didn't "get him" what it was that was so amazing about him. Kind of like you can't explain the beauty of a sunrise.

A sunrise just IS. Alex was natural like that. Elemental, as only the rarest of people are.

BY ROXANNE WARE
Alex's stepmom

Alex skiing with his dad and stepmom.

I have so many memories of Alex. One of the first trips I took with Alex was to a beach house in Bolivar. He was about 11 years old. Blue sky, sunshine, sandy beach, water and lots of exploring. We walked the beach, collected shells, watched sea gulls and talked about whatever came to mind. He was living in Hereford at the time, so the stories were about places and people I would never meet, but he made me laugh as he shared his take on country living.

I think the highlight of that trip was getting to ride the ferry from Bolivar peninsula back to Galveston Island. After all 80+ cars were loaded, the ferry started the 25-minute trip across the Houston ship channel. That's when we got out of the car and went to the top deck. He loved the wind in his face. From there, he could see the dolphins following the ferry. There were dolphins of all sizes, all ages. He loved how they would come alongside the ferry and put on a show, jumping in the air or gliding just below the surface. They were happy, free, and having so much fun.

Then we went downstairs and to the back of the ferry with slices of bread. He threw bread to the seagulls until his arm was tired and the bread was gone. They would not eat out of his hand, but he made them get really close before he threw the bread to them.

I'll always remember him running all over the ferry so that he could see all the action. The dolphins, the seagulls, the waves and the sight of the ferry landing coming into view. He loved the sea breeze in his hair and face. Those were really happy times with that sweet, funny, young boy. We miss him so. . . .

BY NATHAN STONE
Alex's stepdad

Nathan and Alex in Hereford, Texas.

Ready for church on Mother's Day.

Where is your soul?

Are you afraid to die?

Did Jesus know Buddha?

I think the death penalty sucks. Isn't it just murdering a murderer?

Isn't prayer just talking to yourself?

Do churches that baptize by dunking ever think about how much water they waste?

Why are you a carnivore?

What's the deal with cows and Hindus?

What do all of these questions have to do with Alex? These are just a few of the things Alex wondered about. He'd ask these kinds of questions when we were driving or when I was working at the computer—and always out of the blue. As we talked he would listen intently, but I always had the feeling that he already knew the answers. He reminded me of an old soul who had already lived and died many times.

How I do wish he were here so he could see himself in writing. I can also see him smiling that wry smile and wondering what all the fuss is about.

ALEX was very smart, tender-hearted, kind, funny, mysterious, comforting, frustrating, talented, one-of-a-kind.

SCHOOL
ASSIGNMENTS

Alex, fifth grade.

HAPPINESS

Mrs. Barnes' class,
Shirley Elementary, Hereford, Texas

Happiness is . . .

Swimming in a duck pond and getting good grades.

When do you feel happy?

Watching animals (ducks)

What do you like to do when you feel happy?

Sing and talk like an Indian. I would put on comfortable baggy jeans and a baggy night gown. I would watch Animal Planet. I would then become an Indian Duck. My name would be Alex Warehouse the Duck number III. I would live in India and wear a turban. I would eat Spicy Nacho cheese Doritos all day and stay up til 3:01 am I would buy India, Russia, Africa, Alaska and Germany . . . Everything is great and only getting better.

DREAM ISLAND

Once upon a time, there was an island off Thailand called Ko. It does exist, but if I could change it, it would be covered in huge mushrooms, the red and white ones and the neon blue ones. They would be so big I could walk, lay, and sleep on them.

There would be fields of long stem roses with no thorns. Instead of growing out of the dirt, they would grow out of ruby red velvet.

I would live in a Gothic cathedral remodeled into a huge theme palace with one room filled with five feet of plastic balls like Chunky Cheese has.

There would be no bugs except lady bugs. And all kinds of big cats, like leopards, tigers, cheetahs and lions. There would be huge grizzly bears that would love me. And instead of a bed I will sleep on all my pudgy animals. They would all be housetrained and cute. They will eat mocha Frappuccinos from my personal Starbucks.

Whatever I wanted, I would have. I'd just have to say it. There would be orchards of raspberries, peaches and strawberries. That were picture perfect.

There would only be people I like to be there and if something broke or died it would regenerate and a new one would pop up. There would be all types of animals that loved me and I would have all the fun I wanted. No rules, no authority, no boss. Me, my friends and my island of pleasure.

RAINY DAYS

I love rainy days but there are also a lot of bad things too. I will explain some of the good and bad things about a rainy day.

One of the things is it's soothing to the mind, body and soul. I love to read my old books such as Pooh. I like to read them in the garage. I sit in a lawn chair wrapping myself in a warm blanket. I also eat things like Goldfish and chips. Also I like the scent of new fallen rain. The sound eases my troubled mind as well as my soul. It's a very good atmosphere for napping.

There is another reason for liking rainy days, like writing letters, drawing, etc. I like writing letters to friends, family and my pen pal. I draw things like people, places and animals.

There are also a lot of bad things too. One is boredom when there is nothing on TV or nothing on the radio. There's no movies either no books or I wait for something to come up. I can't go outside because it's cold.

Also there are a lot of power outages when it rains. I hate it when I'm in the bathtub and the lights go out. I bump around the bathroom like a fool until the lights come back on. Then everything is completely wet! When I'm watching a suspense thriller when BANG near the end. I also hate not being able to eat microwave things.

I don't like it when I can't go out for recess because it's too muddy. It gets on my nerves when we have to sit inside and do nothing!

So you see there are both good and bad things about rainy days. I preferably like rainy days.

PETS

Pets can be fun but it takes a great deal of responsibility. Taking care of a pet is like having a child. You have to take care of it or it dies.

There are many positive things about having a cat. They purr and lick my hand. When my cat Casey purrs I feel like I did something good. When he licks my hand it makes me laugh because it tickles. Cats require more attention than dogs because they don't show when they're sick. I feel obligated to watch my cats closely. I feel close to my cats so I want to take good care of them. Since my cats make me feel important and happy I want to take care of them.

Dogs are another pet a lot of people have. They have the same basic needs but they need a few different things. I feel since a dog's weight is important. I should take care of that and exercise my dogs. Being around my dogs makes me feel important. Even though there are many good qualities about dogs there are some bad things too. Dogs smell horrible. I hate the smell of dogs. My dog barks at night and I find it annoying. Having a pet is fun and an important part of our lives. Sometimes it's hard, but it's worth it. Pets are fulfilling but they come with great responsibilities.

TEXAS

I will give you some good reasons to come to Texas. Here are the reasons I think you should come to Texas.

There are amazing, historical sites like the Alamo. A lot of Texan soldiers fought for their country. The Alamo was a monastery. It is in San Antonio. It has a historical marker with antique weapons, jewelry and letters. There is also Palo Duro Canyon. The light house is a nice sight to see too. It is in Palo Duro Canyon. There is also a bat cave with cute little fuzzy bats.

There are also friendly people in Texas that will go out of their way for you. They will show you the good restaurants like Underwoods. They have great, wonderful superb mashed potatoes. They have nice warm mouth-watering sourdough rolls. They also have delicious rounded, soft, plump, tender, wonderful award-winning corn. They also have crunchy yummy pickles.

We also have nice hotels like Hilton. It has very fancy crystal chandeliers that light up the ballroom. You get wonderfully marvelous room service too. There is also the Ambassador hotel. It is extremely fancy. It has an indoor fancy pool, restaurant, ballroom and bar. It has a huge lobby and a massive ballroom lit by chandeliers. Ramada is a fancy hotel too. I thought the nachos were superb.

I have told you the reasons you should come to Texas anytime and see everything and explore!

POETRY, NOTES, & DRAWINGS

Alex in his backyard in Hereford, Texas, with his dog, Yellow, and his favorite stuffed animal, Growly.

I AM A FREE SPIRIT

Free spirit is the exact right word because free spirits in most of the world face oppression and every word opposite of freedom. We live many lives and we want to learn and grow from each. Free spirits come into this world to learn how it feels to be the oppressed. How to be yourself and be punished for it. Free spirits in this fleshy world are here to learn what it is like for someone else to take the wheel in their life, to let go and be controlled. I don't however believe that the objective is to be content in being controlled.

I think it is to see how it feels so your soul can expand its compassion, but I think above all that the lesson is how to LOVE YOURSELF. Don't change with the wind, stand strong, when the storm settles, you will be battered and bruised and torn up.

But, you're still standing there. You know you stood your ground, took every fucking blow, and you know what, you survived. That is the moral. No matter what you survived.

Who I Am

Independant
A thinker
neither a leader or folower
spritual
deep
musical
soulful
eclectic
stubborn
unchanging
rediculous

{ Im

silly
dancer
original
outside the box
smart
open minded
big picture oriented
relaxed
insiteful
understanding
questioning
firm in beliefs
rationalizer
caring
creative
in a league of my own
self taught
loyal
honest

RAINBOW

My beautiful, broken rainbow. When I'm around you why do I feel so low? The burning, stinging, ringing in my ears. I hope you know that I can't sleep cause when I do I wake up from the dreams, the dreams that induce my screams that keep me from sleep cause when I do I see you. And I see my dead, grey heart that I don't deserve. You take everything away and leave me to rot and decay. Only me and my fractured rainbow.

As the thick woods of
my cloudy mind grow
I feel less in controll.
I wonder will my soul
heal? I Lie for lies to lies
form the truth of myself
my inner eye a is gouged
my inner ear is torn
my lipps are sewed shut,
My soul is locked my mind
is closed to the public. I'm
looseing my mind, My soul,
my innocence, my morrals
my dignady, my face, my

Self

With Alice in Wonderland
at Disney World, 2000.

1997 – 2000: Poetry, Notes, & Drawings

LOST

But hell was so cold, all the faces are broken, tormented, filled with anguish.

And I'm not attracted to your world, nothing heals, nothing grows. It's lost wandering through Wonderland hand in hand with Alice. Go follow the white rabbit but don't trust him. Don't trust anyone except yourself.

I Bend down to pick a
flower thinking everythings fine
then you see blood down your
palm the thorns tear into my flesh
like razors in the rist of
happyness. The flowers all laugh at
me. Im shuned. the flowars hate me.
want me dead. theres a flowar
conspiracy against me, my soal,
my sainaty. the flowars attacks
my brain.

IMAGINATION

In here my dreams become realities and some of
my realities become dreams
For this is my world of pure imagination. I can alter
change and fit to my
Taste all surroundings. My funhouse of horrors
hounding your mind,
a song that won't go, an ever-present thought, a
never-ending scream,
a recurring dream. Look around and see the
real wonderland.
If you want to see paradise simply look around and
view it,
if you want to change the world there's nothing
to it.

Nightmares to haunt me
Nightmares to kill
Nightmares to comfort me
nightmares to make me think
night mares to keep me awake at night
night mares to wake me up in a cold sweat
night mares to slice blads into my flesh
night mares to save me
night mares to be there
night mares to bleed
night mares I need
nightmares to cringe
nightmares to save
night mares to make you fall
nightmares that make no diffrene at all
night mares they call
night mares at night
nightmares to hide me
night mares to be my friend

TRUTH

Most everything you deny, the truth to yourself
usually is what you need to hear,
What you seek.
This is a proficiency only people of the truth
could understand.
Not me, not you, but us.
There will be a unity between me and my spirit.
I can tap into my dark side or my light and
mischievous side.
My dark fantasy or my free rambunctious self.

your eyes see. soe much
yet so little. you think every
thing is clear yet its foggy,
and blurd. so Hide the world,
so hide the truth, so hide
our Minds in your Hell. Is this
My life. did you program me?
am I a ~~lazy~~ malfunkison? a glich?
nothing is true
nothing is true
nothing is true
nothing is true
nothing is true
nothing is true
nothing is true
nothing is true
nothing is true
nothing is true
and it's all a Lie.

I love your smile
I hate the things it hides
I hate that way you smile
I hate the way you make me feel

I hate myself
I hate the way i feel
I hate the grades i make
I hate the way i see myself
I hate it that I hate you.

Alex Was ~~You~~ make me happy

WHY?

I will eat no meat,

Nor milk or eggs.

I made a pledge not to harm

Animals were here to look up to and enjoy.

Why must they be so cruel to true beauty?

Why must they kill and mutilate God's gift?

Why, I ask myself? Why, why, why?

Now the only thing I can do is hope.

All I can do is cry.

All I can do is try to make it stop.

For all we know they could be family.

Why does it happen?

I ask myself every day.

Could it be human error?

Is it not a sin?

Thou shall not kill.

Thou shall not steal. (Life, meat, head, skin)

This runs through my mind all the time.

Why? I wonder, *why, why, why?*

How can we do this? *How?*

I thought
I was
wrong

I thought I loved you
I thought I needed you
I thought I ~~ever~~ wanted
this. I thought You cared
I Thought you could
change me I thought
Then Every thing was
I thought it was real
It felt real, anyway.
Now I'm lost. I'm oh
so hopeless. You are gone
without even being here
And I still need you
And I still want you
and I still want this
But Your gone And I'm
still right here. So
I'll stay here on my
sickly thrown. My dreams
distroyed.

TO BRITTANY

You are the beauty in my dark, damp life. I feel as though I could drown in the depth of your kind welcoming soul. Your elegant beauty fulfills me. Your passion, your love, you are but a rose in a mile of weeds. You are true. You are cruel. You are passionate. You make me want to be better. You are the piece of the puzzle that I have never found until now. You complete me. You are the sole thing that fills me with warm sunshine and rainbows. You are the one. You are true. You are kind. You are fair. You are my soul mate. You are a part of me now.

the decay

The decay that eats away.
The decay that wont go away.
The decay is all I have today.
The decay that tear my dreams
The decay infesting in my skin away.
The decay wants to get in
The decay that allways wins
The decay that knows no ends.
The decay that is so mystical
The decay that is hypricrital
The decay that is sadistical
The decay that took all my dreams
the decay that induces all my screams
the decay that is riping at the seams
the decay that lies so it seems
the decay wants more, by all means
the decays steals all my dreams
the decay is vishious & malishious
~~the decay is wicked~~
the decay that is so pretenious

The freeing of a dove
showes the beauty of Love
Hate Love And Love hate
Hide your feelings for they
will take them all away
You try to mend the broken
mind but its all too late
You hurt me you did nothing
but betray. Beauty is so
agly through my fals broken
eyes. You hopelessly fill me
up with all your broken lies.
god damn I wish I
could see and god damn
I wish I could be
All thoes twisted, fucken,
fk.broken, thoughts that
you Made me belive.
But I know you lied.
And dear god I know I tried.

I developed a cold
and didnt let you in
so you told me I had Polio
Your only son of sin.
You told me that you
loved me, as you forced
me in my iron lung
And tied me down, so that
I couldnt run.
I only had a cough,
now I have terminal disease,
untill I actnaly got polio
and couldnt even breath.
I had a small ailment,
that you solved with a curse,
and couldnt understand,
why I was only getting worse.
You soon got tired,
and realized I had nothing
at all, so you thought
i didnt have polio
as you unplugged me
from the wall.

I am lost in a maze
of darkness with no light,
no exit, searching for
A glimmer of light a door that
opens to a outside. I have
ben in the darkness so long
my eyes have ben blinded
my darkness. I'm lost, scared,
renning from darkness in wich
surrounds me. unable to
ecape. I hear nothing. I see
nothing. I smell nothing I feel
only the Icy cold walls.
my body frozen, raw wanting
out feeling like a trapt
cornerd animal. No one
can save me, my mind,
my saneity. But do-
do try. It Amases me.

I'm only happy when I dream
But I'm an insomniac
Its my only release
Untill I wake up and
realise where im at

porciline sunrise
and im fragile in the morning
sun comes up and
I start mourning
you must believe the pain i feel
but the complicity of it all
just builds you a shield
I'm sure where working equal
When you stole away my life
they gave you a fucking handbook
but your doing whats "right"
you say its 50/50
but you know it isnt close
but you expect me to be
happy giving me pills to
not be monrose

you say you stick to your guns
but I have the bullets
all you have is a trigger
but im the one to pull it.

'TIL THE DAY I DIE

It's too late

God's irate

I've got too many people doing cat's cradles with

my veins

Crying in vain

Hard to explain

The knot in my

Stomach

Or the excruciating pain

I miss you when I

Fall asleep

I miss you when

I breathe

I miss you as soon

As I get up

I miss you because

You're what

I need

I miss you

When I close my

Eyes

I miss you when

I feel deprived

I feel you

When I feel alive

I'll miss you

'Til the day I die

I'm liveing in a ~~mirror~~
mirror everythangs backwards,
everythangs confused, my mind
will not stop raceing, my
body will not go my voice
is useless everything's letting
go. I, out of my mind
am a running through my rotting
dreams against a force unstopable,
uncontroable eating my flesh,
my brans, my insides. feasting
on my fath, morials. I feel
myself sleping away. I am my own
slave in a life of guilt.
I sell my soal for pills
to make it go-away.
My own fire burs my flesh
makeing my blood set on
fire like oil. Is this me?

My life is a huge fucken
circle. I think, I know, I lern
yet it won't go away. It is
burned into my mind why!
cant! I. forget! My mind is
breakeing.

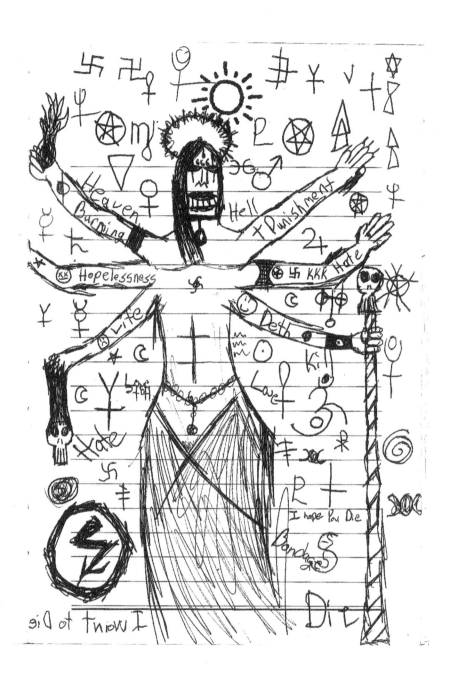

MY DARK AND TWISTED
THOUGHTS

My nightmares pour out of the tips of my finger in

A wrath of evil with no mercy, killing and destroying

Anything in its way.

These are the hellish experiences that erupt inside

My twisted head. Sometimes they overcome me like

A wave of lava over a city burning.

The decay of the world is beginning and the Anti-

Christ

Is coming, coming here.

I so often find myself pondering the corners of the

Universe looking for an exit that doesn't exist.

I need a crutch to lean on. That is why I search

through

So many things that don't work. It's a bunch of

bullshit

And so am I.

Why? I find myself asking my brain. *Why* and *why* over

Make me wonder because all it says back is, "I don't know."

I make myself sick trying to make myself look deeper

Inside my scabbed cut shell.

It has an eternal flame that burns me and others around me.

My secrets humor the eyes of the ones who have interest.

What evil can corrupt a man in such a way that he is a robot?

What does it mean? Can anyone answer that? Maybe so.

Now I find myself in a trance where anything oozes out

Like blood through a cough that never ends.

I feel sick at the theory that people can help. What a lie!

Sometimes I lie to feel secure of my own dignity.

The end of my life is only being there is a way out
where

You escape, enlightenment, heaven, call it what you
wish

It is the thought that matters.

My palms feel a piercing pain like a stake through
my hand.

Why Why Why Why Why Why Why Why Why

I have my tears to
keep me company
because im on my own
I have your love
when I'm loveless
on my own
I have your
loving touch
as I ccress my
brokin skin
and touch and see
whats going out
but cant get anything
in.
I cant concieve
your acts of love
their tearing at
my soul
with broken bones
tore off my throare
Im homsick with no
home
I'll be your nothing
doing just that
going no where

So many people
with so much to say
So many dollars that
you are throwing away
I understand who your
trying to save
but that person isnt
me, And to be, that person
I'm not as brave
Velvet sunrise
and thorns in my sides
and reasons
not worth reasoning to stay alive
the antidote for the problem
you thought was me
Was too strong for me
and the repercutions it
caused where too damaging
to concieve.
I'm choked up on pain
and inable to breath
and feeding on the need
to escape and be free.
because you could never
understand the idea that is
me,

BELIEVE

Beyond forest, beyond trees, beyond love, beyond needs,
beyond the hate and what it feeds.
Live up to falling down
beyond the urge of waiting to drown.
Open a music box and cut away.
Reach inside for reasons to stay,
becoming one running away,
coming together to get away,
it hides the hurt, it hides the pain,
help me love you, sweet decay.
Hurt yourself, get away,
find yourself, decide to stay.
A cut, a wound, a reason why,
A promise, a person, a meaningless lie.
Find a way to make me feel,
find a way to make me heal,
find a way to make it real.
Need some love, need some pain,
there is no difference, it's all the same.
Nothing to lose, nothing to gain,
everything is nothing, nothing is vain.

Nothings what it seams the ~~begins~~ Fakeness
of my raw self can only be
exposed in my ~~a~~ writeing
in wich inriches my ~~my~~ hevy
damp seal. It manifests causeing
me to feel as thow my
bones and organs are rotting.
~~So~~ ~~it~~ what will save you? It?
It inwich dragg you into its
sick-twisted hell? Tunning you
in to a potted dead corps
By feeding uppon your dignedy
respect for your self, your sanegity.
go away leave me alone dont
mess with me no! no! no!
No! no! No!
no

SITTING BY THE SEA

A little girl, sitting by the sea, friends drowning in the oceans,

too tied down to flee.

She couldn't even see her friends, "the ocean was bad to me"

Sometimes she wants to die and go along with her friends

It's never fun enough till all the fun ends.

Run away Gemini, you're tied down, watch you fly,

pick you up, watch you die.

Mark of Pisces in your skin,

watch the salt water, bleeding in.

A little girl on the river flowing, going, slowing down

flying, freed, too afraid to drown.

Weeping by the sea, cigarette burning into her skin,

falling away, finally getting in

She's torn between her two best friends in the

beginning, and the one in the end.

The one in a needle, the one in the skin, the one who

bounces off. The one who gets in

scars of a wasted life, dripping with sin.

Scars from wasted time, coming from within.

I need the smell of you, all becomes clear

A fantasy I live, all becoming clear.

The pain that I have showed, all coming back to here

THE DOWNFALL OF SOCIETY

The downfall of society and the rise is when it is down it will become united.

I think that fate will sort us out in deliverance

In the beginning everything was old.

In the beginning is when they stole your soul.

In the beginning we have nothing to see.

In the beginning we have nothing to behold.

In the beginning we started out so cold.

I believe in beauty

I believe in faith

I believe we are ugly and unworthy to be saved

I believe in nothing

I believe it's true

I never asked to become like you.

VANILLA LACE

Everything went when you walked through that
door

A soft embrace

A soft noise as I hit the floor

A slut, a used, a whore.

No matter how much I have I always want more

No matter my hate of this I always want more

Never happy, never happy anymore.

Tears running down my face

"Vanilla lace"

Taste like salt

You make me feel

Like I'm the one

At fault

When he thinks everything I say is lies

It's always funny to wonder how you

Look through other people's eyes.

This boy he can't be good enough

No matter how hard he tries

Sitting in a car of flies

Can't help feeling disappointed

Can't help feeling hurt

Can't help these feelings

Can't help but feel

Can't cut

Can't heal.

Showed you the obvious

Too blind to see

Too bored to steal

Go to church to kneel

Help me satisfy myself

"kinda pretty and red"

the mushrooms of white
and all, red fuck you all
up in your head listn
to the colers and see
the air and, feel the
sky that I am blowing
a kiss to . there is
only me, the feelings and
you. so place it on
your tounge and inhale
bottoms up and take
a pill haven fun
and feelin the music
bring it on and get your
fill

NEVER ENOUGH

cant cut

cant heal

cant hurt

cant feel

a dream of silence

a dream of something I made

a dream of something thats real

a dream of something that wont fade

want to try

want to be

want truth

want to be free

try to feel

try to cry

try to live

try to be free

need your touch

need your kiss

need it all

need all of this

ill never be good enough for you . . .

Rest for the ever abused mind.
Rest for the stomoch that is forever
vomiting. Rest for eyes that see so
much they arn't intentid to see.
Rest for the silence that is
used too much. Rest for the
angry voices in my head in wich
never mute. Rest for my cut,
bleeding flesh ~~which~~ filters
my rage and pain. Rest for the
sleepless and torn, Rest for the
soal inwich is so battered. Rest
for the guilt inwich dosent go.
Rest for. the reaching arms.
Rest thats all. Rest for the
tearfull. Rest for the fearless.
Rest, is it to much? Rest
for the never ending, Lies,
Rest for the fucking, world!

1997 – 2000: Poetry, Notes, & Drawings

I LIKE MY CAT . . .
AND OTHER NOTES

I like my cat.

The happiest time was when I got my cat.

I want to know how much longer till the human race dies off.

Back home there are some woods.

I regret everything.

At bedtime I go to bed.

Boys play sports.

The best time is at night.

What annoys me are hunters.

People do bad things.

A Mother is supposed to be loving.

I feel angry.

My greatest fear is people watching me.

In high school I will get a car.

I can't be very social.

Sports are pointless, except for a few.

When I was a child my brother let me fall on my head.

My nerves get jumped on a lot, like a trampoline.

Other people judge other people.

I suffer from a slight case of paranoia.

I failed in pleasing a lot of people.

Reading books makes me sleepy.

My mind is a maze, a very confusing one, with no doors.

The future is something I don't think about a lot.

I need a lot of space.

Marriage is beautiful but it can be boring.

I'm best when I'm not under stress.

Sometimes I stare at things.

What pains me is seeing animals suffer.

I hate a lot of things.

This school is in Hereford.

I am very boring.

The only trouble I get in is for expressing my views.

I wish I could get away from everything in the world.

My father is a dancer and a good one.

I secretly put spells on people.

I like making poetry.

Dancing is one of the things I'm good at.

My greatest worry is for people to think about me too much.

Most girls are too full of themselves.

SELECTIONS
from 2000 – 2003

≫≪

13 – 16 YEARS OLD
Coe Academy, Waco, Texas
Waco High School, Waco, Texas

Alex at his dad's house on Turtle Creek.

REFLECTIONS

Homer Airport, Alaska. By Corrina Pariyar.

Homer, Alaska, 2002

BY KAREN BERGER
Alex's Aunt "Ken Ken"

I've done such a good job of dodging this letter because I'm most afraid of what will pour out of me. The role of aunt does not get too much guidance in the grief and processing department, and over the last eleven years I have gone from sad to mad with a great deal in between and back around again. Being the stoic Altman, I've felt it best to just keep the hurt inside and live on "let it go."

I've read Alex's words and, honestly, it stirred up more of the anger I feel than the love. Just reading and trying to piece together the life of Alex and what it meant to his mom, his friends, and family still hits me with the less than positive feelings. I have to make myself remember he had a disease. Mental health and our family have some deep roots. I believe his disease killed him, not himself. With just enough dumb-ass 19-year-old added to it, that made it happen.

I wish something more profound could bubble up, but my thoughts go dark. All of the "what ifs" and "if onlys" jump to the front of my mind. But I'm happy about this project. It is a great collaboration between Alex and his family and friends.

BY CORRINA PARIYAR

A close friend of Alex in Homer, Alaska

Alex with Corrina in Alaska.

I've written so many things, but I think this is what I'd like to share. How hard an exercise in grief and grace!

Alex was full of love. In him I saw the Beloved. To remember him is to remember love. But also with love is loss. The suffering that accompanies losing someone so full of love can only be soothed with metaphor and knowing someday suffering transcends to grace.

I'm amazed we had the courage to find each

other in life together. Alex and I became fast and immediate friends, as if we'd known each other all along. I think it's because we both understood there is more to life than "living." There's a side to life not many understand nor want to—the beauty in death and the connection in sorrow. Art and spirituality are born in these dark, hard places. I think that's why I still feel him with me, even though we knew each other in such a brief moment.

I remember funny details of our friendship. Simple things: the walks we took, the day adventures. These simple memories make me smile completely. One afternoon, we wanted to make a fire on the beach, but we didn't really think it through. We wanted to make s'mores, and after we couldn't start a fire of our own we wandered over to another woman's fire. She was inside her camper and came out when she saw us. We pretended we weren't from Alaska and I think we convinced her that we were a newly married couple. I remember she was wearing pink sweats. I can't remember everything that was said, but Alex had a great accent, and it was so much fun to pretend that we were together on vacation seeing Alaska for the first time.

I need to always try to be thankful for the gift of our friendship. And although he took his own life, I do believe he took it somewhere. Suffering still comes from my wanting more of what was, clinging to that past. Alex is part of my past but he is also present in me today and will be tomorrow.

BY BECKY WARREN

One of Alex's teachers at Waco High School

Becky with Alex.

Fun Alex, impish Alex, frustrating Alex, mischievous Alex, lovable Alex. Alex knew when he had pushed my last buttons but would end up making me laugh. He was the only student I ever had who could get away with calling me "sugar britches." Well, no one has ever called me that! Whenever he would say that, I was always caught off guard and would dissolve into laughter. And he would again escape my wrath.

He was, in my mind, a happy and funny guy who was passionate about a lot of things and had plans to see his dreams into fruition. He seemed to thrive socially and enjoyed the raves he attended. So much energy!

I think he instinctively recognized my deep sorrow, having lost my daughter just a few years before meeting him. He kept me on my toes, in stitches, and in the present. I knew he had his own demons, but I did not have the skill or the fortitude to exorcise those. I wish I had been more aware of how dangerously close those demons were.

I will always miss his impish smile and radiant energy. He was a dreamer; I wish he had been able to attain those dreams and keep us all laughing.

BY AUDRA HALL
Alex's first girlfriend

Alex and Audra.

2000 – 2003: Reflections

Everything between Alex and I was always top secret. We snuck out. We lied. We did everything we weren't supposed to do. Most of it was his idea, but not all of it.

I had always been a goody-two-shoes, and I was dying of boredom. It was eating up the good parts of me. Alex saved me from the monotony of my impoverished and academic-driven life, and I tried to help him bridge the emotional gaps he had with his parents and encourage him to do his homework in between the rule breaking.

I can't count how many times I told him, "If you do what they want, then you get to do what you want." I always felt like I would never be good enough, but Alex made sure that I knew I was perfect just the way I was.

Alex always felt like he was undeserving of love. I just let him be himself, and I loved him just the way he was, or however he wanted to pretend to be from day to day.

My mom didn't like very many of my friends, but Alex amused her and made her laugh, and he was always welcome at our house. I wish he was still here.

I think he'd be thrilled to know that gay marriage is legal, that marijuana is legal in several states, that the electronic dance music scene is alive and in full force, and that there are a lot more Tim Burton movies to watch. I wish that he could have seen a little further into the future, because I think he would have liked it.

All I needed were six more months and I would have been inviting him to stay in my apartment in Dallas and get out of Waco. Time was not on our side.

Alex is always going to be a part of me. I will continue to break all the rules. I promise.

BY JILL DULOCK WIMBERLEY

Alex's friend in Waco, Texas

Jill watches as Alex opens gifts at his high school graduation party, 2004.

There is so much that could be said. Alex was deep and layered.

The first time I met him was through my best friend, Audra. She had moved the year before to a new school and met Alex at Waco High. The first image I remember of him is seeing a really skinny, tall kid sitting cross-legged on the floor making "candy bracelets." These were just simple plastic bead bracelets. He had a pile of already-made ones sitting on the floor and before the evening was done he had given me more than a few.

It wasn't just me he gave them to; he gave them to everyone. One time, we were at a football game being crazy and dancing in the stands when he noticed a police officer watching us from below. Did he ignore him or maybe confront him? Nope. He took him a candy bracelet and tried to befriend him.

He was so giving it shocked me. You always hear about people who would give the shirt of their back, but Alex really would. I saw him do it once at a party after someone threw up on theirs at a party. We were almost always at a party. We called ourselves "crunk-a-lunks." We were always crunk and looking for fun! We found it very often. He also often "found the floor" or found himself knocking on random people's doors when he drank too much.

Alex had to be going or doing or planning all the time. He got so sad if he was alone or not doing anything. If he wasn't dancing or drinking or being crazy, his whole emotional state collapsed. I think this is why he was always pushing for bigger badder better fun! I am not going to lie. I couldn't keep up with him sometimes. I spent so much time taking care of him, retrieving his shoes that he threw out a car window while we were driving down Lake Shore Drive with Andrew, telling him he couldn't just knock on random doors at two in the morning trying to find more people to drink with us, and hiding his keys so he couldn't drive home drunk.

He spent most of his time trying to get me to be not "repressed," something he called me from the first day I met him. Sometimes he won, and we all got crazy! Sometimes I won, and he had to cancel his plans for later because I thought he was too drunk to drive.

I never was as outgoing or trusting or loving as Alex was. He had a hug for everyone. I didn't really enjoy people in my space, but he was persistent. It didn't take long for me to love an Alex hug, and it took even less time for him to become one of my closest friends.

He gave me great guy advice and instigated my first kiss and date with my now husband, Justin. I'm pretty sure he told me for months to forget any other guys that were interested in me and concentrate on Justin. I'm glad I eventually listened to him because almost fourteen years later, we have an amazing life and three beautiful kids, one of which we named after Alex.

I turned to him many times in my darkest days. He comforted me many times when I thought life's difficulties were more than I could bear. I can still hear him say "find comfort in my bosom" and picture his skinny arms pulling my head against his chest as he comforted me a million times. It doesn't seem fair that someone who was key in seeing me through depression and bad times isn't here to see the other side with me. I'll always wonder what incredible things the world lost when we lost him, but I'll also always treasure the five years and millions of memories I have! PLUR (Peace, Love, Unity, Respect).

Jill with her daughter, Alex.

BY AMY WARE
Alex's sister-in-law

There were a number of times Alex expressed interest in my religious beliefs. It was apparent he was searching for answers, and I shared what I knew, which at that time wasn't much. Once, he and his friend, Taylor, came to a Passover celebration my mother hosted. I remember his friend, Taylor, being asked to read an excerpt from Psalms. She made the peaceful moment a memorable one when she pronounced Psalms as "Palms." Alex was quick to help his friend feel better by confessing his own confusion of Biblical words. We all had a good laugh and enjoyed the fresh perspective the two offered.

BY SALEM MCKENNA WARE

Alex's niece

I was young, and I don't remember much. But there is this one memory that, for some reason, is still vaguely clear. A zoo trip. We'd gone to the zoo for the day, and, to be completely honest, I couldn't even tell you if we saw any animals. But we had so much fun. We played, and we joked. At one point, for some reason or another, I'd even dipped my head in the stream to cool off and Alex held me up so I didn't fall in. We bonded – just as any uncle and his niece would.

Alex with his nieces, K'lee and Salem.

Alex's niece, K'Lee, wearing her Uncle Alex shirt.

SCHOOL
ASSIGNMENTS

Bio-Poem

Alex

tall, skinny, silly, and baked

related to to all man kind

who cares about the love

who feels blowed

who needs tampi

who gives hugs

who fears grumps

who would like to see Jerry Garcia

Resident of TX

Haiku

bleeding from within
merlot staining the faces of friends
dripping on the banks

Cornbread McGallahad

I once knew a man named
Cornbread McGallahad he excelled
in the business of seeds.

He lived in a house, rather
close to the sea. His seed
business took care of their
needs.

He smoked all the time, and
had a sweet-tooth for wine
And made himself quite prone
for disease.

Turtle
CREEK

A
Mountain View & A walk away
from A garden of
Peace

great! 9/

I
Love this
House Plan
& What he felt
good part of
his life

Take a right at the peace
garden and you head down
the road to turtle creek.

1   So much Ivy, vines, shade, cover.
     the darkest house on the block.
     Walk around the <u>deck</u> to a
     steep, lush, glowing mesh of visual
2   aliveness, the constant flow of
     water, carving an escape rou-
     back to the lake.

3   I always thought it was a
     bit of competitive humor, me vs.
     the home security. I could get
     in my house without a key
     through a slidelock and a
     wedge or two. I came over
     when the house was left alon
     Broke in to my own home.
     And sometimes if not most
     of the time brought my
     reletives that dont share my
     blood. We had fun, rebelling
     against sadness, apathy, and
     buying the hooliganation of youth
     We may have been hooligens
     but it was by choice not
     appointment.

4

the kitcian was always stocked
with good grocries, the
parishables where usually
past date, but when he
came back the new would
come too. Midnight, food fights,
licquor uppon our breath. We
tried to muffle the inner
joy for fear of waking up
the sleeping.

5

My dad won the big screen
televsion in a competative
swing danceing ~~competition~~
~~collection~~. Trip to a nameless
myrtle beach, Galveston, or Dallas.
We had a 200 CD changer over
crowded with toe tappin beats.
We had a dance floor put
in before we hard wood floored
the whole house. My dad was
& still is a religious dancer
and devout at that. He did
routienes with an assortment of
women, usually as flashy & cequined
as he was. There was a big
fire in the fireplace when it
was cold and I wanted to
make one. Aside from the
required Hallmark Christmas
icons.

lots of
good detail!

6 You could wash up for the
   day, or; wash off the nights
   tireing trasspasses. The master
7 bathroom enjoys the pleasure
   of reservation from outside
   Souls.

L My room, My suite, My perminent
   rent house, Private, to an extent...
L personal experiment. - A great
   Vantage point to hear the snoring
   guerentee of unconcious sleep.
   The door's absence of squeeks
   help the incontent sneak out
   of the paradise I seeap into.
   when im homesick on the weekends.

8 My father has always had a
   weakness for shopaholism.
   Quantity over quality, All of the
   enganeered closet space in the
   house wouldnt do. So he
   hung up beams in the other
   room and turned it into a
   closet too.

9 My Memories of the Master
   bed where always made
   except the far right side
   which, for sleep, came undone.
   The only other perminant resident
   of the King sized bed
   was an enormous jovial

Cat named Bŏzēe

Outside the White walls and
tiles, was the Devine Green
House, I could plug in one
electronic Unit for our pleasure
& comfort, It happened on
a snow day in texas. We gathered
together in commune in the
safty of the greenhouse. We
sat shivvering not so scilently,
The space heater sat lifeless,
next to the boom box that
gave birth to the sutle truth
of bob Marly. You could
see the love in the eyes
feeling back across through
the enclosed haze, into my
soul. Both of my mates that
body heated the snow day,
Became the trend of winter.
And, judged, sentenced, and
carried out their own fates.
Got all tied up in the ropes
of reality, and got a gravity
lesson.

Bozee watches over the
house in spirit, Permanently
imBedded in the soil of
turtle creek, The escape route
of choice for One stream, atleast.

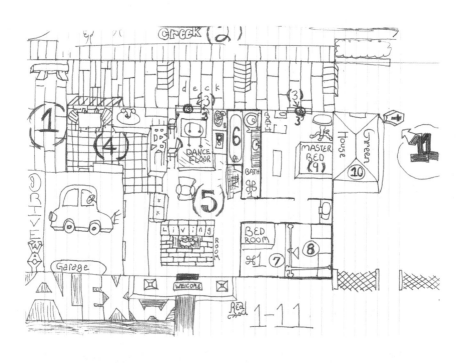

At a rave with a friend, Fernando Rogers, 2002.

RAVES

Raves have a bad rap by most people who listen to "concerned parents." They seem to think that you only go to raves to take drugs and have sex. That's one of the many incorrect ideas surrounding raves. Another that the security turns their heads when they see drug use. If this is so then why are people arrested at raves?

The other thing that is incorrect is the list of paraphernalia. Glow sticks have nothing to do with drugs. You dance with them.

I have to say the most unbelievable cause of concern was a bottle of water. I want to get the "concerned parents" out on a dance floor for twelve hours and see who wants a bottle of water. People should take the time to understand. This is the rave culture.

The people who attend raves are mostly in their teens. They usually range from twelve to about thirty, but can be up to sixty. It's a big variety of cultures, race, and sexual orientation.

The look is very colorful and childish. Popular items of dress are Sailor Moon, SpongeBob's SquarePants, Powerpuff Girls, Anime, Teletubbies, and Blue's Clues. The pants are usually big and covered in hanging glow sticks. Beads are among the most

---

popular item. They are little, plastic beads on elastic string.

Most people get there by driving or riding the bus. An Austin rave for someone in Waco would be about $25.00 bus fare, $30.00 per ticket, and $30.00 for food, water and other stuff. The rave tickets vary from $15.00 to VIP tickets which are $95.00. It depends on how much you're willing to spend.

Yes, there are drugs at raves these include X which is a mixture of methamphetamine and LSD. There's also acid (a hallucinogen). There's no alcohol or marijuana. They are depressants and you can't dance if you're depressed. Techno dancing is a fast aerobic dance. There are drugs but they don't push them. The people there are friendly and nice. They just say, "You want some whatever?" And if you shake your head, they go away. People don't come to raves to do drugs. They come to dance and get lost in the music. The main two drugs are scenery drugs that enhance the music. The people who use drugs at raves usually are to celebrate not escape.

They play mostly techno on the stages but some stages play Jungle, hip-hop, Reggae, and bass line. Techno is electronic music that can be made and remade to form different kinds of songs. Its electronic sounds like synth vocals and piano. It's always repetitive so even after you leave you can still hear and feel the music.

Jungle is slow sounds of nature with techno mixed in. Island music is also mixed this way. Bass line is bass beats rhythmically with fast short beats in the background. This music is aimed at getting you lost in the beat and forgetting your problems.

My first time at a rave was when I was in Houston. We picked up my best friend at the bus station. That night we went to the rave at The Freedom World Ranch. There were security people everywhere. I had to wait in a line for an hour. I could hear the bass. They frisk you then let you buy a ticket and go in. When I got in the rave I went to the vendors and bought a necklace. We went to look at all the stages. I stayed at the main stage most of the night. They had the two main DJs 2-live crew and Paul Oakenfold.

Raves are an interesting culture. People coming together to have fun. People need this. In all the excitement about raves and their association with drugs, no one seems to look at the positive side of raves. Raves are a place for outcasts to join in a place of freedom and comfort in a place where everyone's a friend and there's no trouble. You usually can't achieve this in any other environment. It can cheer you up and help.

Raves are an outlet for people to come out and go all out. You can party for twelve hours. You can watch the lights or look over and see someone dancing. If you jump and spin and move your arms you feel like you are a professional dancer. The little dance you do when you hear your favorite song at home you can do there. They're almost addictive because once you go to one you want to go every chance you get.

Raves are artistic in the minds of creative individuals, a place or outlet where your creative feeling can roam wild. While the bass weighs heavy on your chest, it is a place almost enlightening, a fantasy, a place where music is the language and everybody is in charge. Almost falling away from your body I like the comfort it provides. Nothing but happiness and people who are either enjoying or running from life.

The DJ controls the life of the party. Like a puppet master, his turntables are cables and the music is the pull on the strings and the beat carries your body. Everything is distorted; bright and colorful lights reflect off the smoke from the smoke machines. The smell of smoke the sweat and the broken glow sticks and the people dancing and kicking up dirt all combine to make it unforgettable.

There is not an easy way to describe the feeling that you get from mass dance with strobes and blaring beats. The most comfortable feeling and the most colorful people make it almost impossible to resist the party. The music, it fills you up and never lets you go.

I see from the corners of my eyes the smiles on their

faces. I look around and I see the glowing energy in the way that the people dance. Once the bass fills your bones then you can't stop dancing.

"We're here for the music, the dancing is just a side effect." Electronic music is making its way into the mainstream with sounds like synth mixed with voices and pianos. This is found in most every type of music. If you have a program which gets outcasts and prom queens to coexist peacefully it's probably a good thing. It's a chance for a multitude of people to come together around their love of music, dancing and techno. Instead of gangs, hate and violence, you come to be peaceful in a place of creative freedom. You also get to see people from different cultures. But not everything about raves is good. There are bad things too. These are more easily noted by the press. A lot of people crammed into one small place with high emotions can be dangerous. There's also a threat of drugs.

As you can see there's more to raves than drug abuse and sex.

AND We're All Just suicide kings waiting in vein for that split second of deliverance...

Pull my trigger... Bang.
And the whole world
faded Away.
see god in a handgun
and life in a
flame.

MARILYN MANSON: ANTICHRIST OR MODERN PROPHET?

I think that Marilyn Manson is a hero of our time.

What is a prophet? It isn't a fortuneteller or somebody who predicts the future. In a biblical sense a prophet was someone who pushed the edges of a lazy culture stretched people's minds irritated the status quo, and saw things that most people couldn't or wouldn't see.

Well, well! Who else fits that category? Gandhi, Martin Luther King, Jr., and even Jesus. They all had the same type of thinking. And that is why we admire them.

So choose for yourself as we go into the life and mind of Marilyn Manson. Antichrist or modern prophet?

His mother, Barb, and father, Hugh Warner, didn't know that their innocent, shy, Christian, child would grow up to be one of the biggest controversies in America. He attended church and went to Heritage Christian School.

He was always worrying. He started to believe his teacher that told them the Apocalypse was coming because Reagan (who was President at the time) had six letters in his first, middle, and last names. He was told that this was the absolute truth and it couldn't be interpreted in any other way.

He became so involved that he started to have nightmares that continue to this day. Nightmares about the fall of the world and the Antichrist. He started reading books on the subject and watching movies such as, *The Exorcist, The Omen,* and *A Thief in the Night.*

His Christian upbringing (which he would later reject) scared him. He was intimidated by all of it and it made him feel trapped.

In his autobiography, *The Long Hard Road Out of Hell* (ReganBooks, HarperCollins Publishers, New York; 1998), he says, "I was a Episcopalian which is basically a diet Catholic." (p.19) His church (school) was scary for him. Here he encountered a person to be idolized (the minister) who was touching people inappropriately and making them scream and cry. He didn't understand.

He was picked on for being skinny. He was picked on for having different ideas. But soon he would become "Marilyn Manson."

By the time he was 17 years old he had accepted his pen name, Marilyn Manson. Okay, let me start from the beginning of his journey to fame.

He started a band and made all the members choose a celebrity icon first name and a serial killer for a second. The band was called, "Marilyn Manson and the Spooky Kids." This was back before he shaved off his eyebrows. This was the late eighties and early nineties.

The band would change: whether it be new band members, a new sound, or a new look. The group really wasn't a band as such. It was just a bunch of teen boys playing freaky music and recording them having stupid conversations.

After their first record, "Smells Like Children," went on the market (and flopped) he decided he wanted to make music that included lyrics written by the band. And they wanted to send out a message that said to the world: "We're tough!"

They wrote, "Portrait of an American Family," that depicts acts of violence and suicide This caught the eye of people and while some thought of him as a person to fear they also thought he might be just a fad. People would soon find out that he was anything but a fad.

Their first record to hit big was "Antichrist Superstar." In "Anthem Sounds of the Beautiful People," screaming, loudness, and controversy fueled the record. Even the name makes most people feel uncomfortable.

He recorded a follow-up album entitled, "Mechanical Animals," that was more of a mainstream rock album. His figure in this album is Omega (pronounced "Omega"): a drug-numbed sample of soul.

The CD depicted mind-numbing drugs, joyless sex, and gay cops. This had two songs that got airplay on most main rock stations: "Dope Show," and "I don't like the Drugs but the Drugs like Me."

The latest album, "Holy Wood," has also stirred controversy. The cover shows Marilyn Manson, crucified and missing his lower jaw. This album was made after the Columbine thing. He wanted to show that the Crucifixion is also an act of violence and the jaw missing is a symbol of censorship.

Who knows what's next for this man of shock.

There have been at least ten items of controversy in Marilyn Manson's career.

Yes, he makes us uncomfortable, and yes, he is controversial. But in all of this maybe he just wants people to think. Think about themselves and their surroundings. And maybe learn about what makes us the corporate, conglomerate, American world he depicts and detests.

Sources:

"A Portrait of the Rock Star as a Young Worm," by Daryl Fougnie; April 29, 1999 @ www.albion.edu.

The Long Hard Road Out of Hell; Marilyn Manson with Neil Strauss; ReganBooks, HarperCollins Publishers: New York, NY; 1998)

The Diary of Marilyn Manson, MTV

~~Nightmare~~ wet dream on elm street. ✓

Ⓥ 10

✗ I once knew
a gal named Jesible
Sam who sat
in a scarlet lit
district, she'd pick
up a man, take
money from his
hand, and tell
him just where
to stick it.
(the money that is)

Don't change

Limerick -
Nice use of rhythm

VEGETARIAN MEAL PLAN

Health class

I was reading online a publication from the American Dietetic Association to find out the best way to have a healthy vegetarian diet. I have to look this stuff up because I cook vegetarian soul food that would give someone with heart problems their toll tag to the pearly gates.

So with this said, you're supposed to consume six servings of grain, three to five servings of vegetables, two-four servings of fruit, and five to seven ounces of beans, nuts, or meat alternatives. A few of the ways I try to eat healthy are as follows.

I eat balance bars as snacks, drink energy drinks and eat a wide variety of food. Balance bars taste good and have a lot of vitamins and protein in them. Red Bulls give me energy to exercise.

My favorite type of ethnic food is Indian (dots, not feathers). Indian food is mostly vegetarian because the vast majority of India are vegetarian Hindus. So it has a lot of complete proteins like chickpeas and curry over rice. Curry and hot pepper are good for your immune and digestive system.

I cook a lot of tofu. It's not exactly healthy but it tastes good and has protein. I serve it with black beans and rice. I deep-fry it in vegetable oil with chili powder and cumin as well as some other spices. Make beans with onions, peppers, and other seasonings. Serve it over brown rice and sometimes I put in on tortillas.

I'm a big fan of trashy food so that provides me with my sodium, SpaghettiOs. To be a healthy vegetarian, you have to eat a wide variety of foods and not mind trying new things.

Alex's vegetarian grocery list.

POETRY, NOTES,
& DRAWINGS

NORTHERN STAR

Infinity is a thin string binding two empty hollows

I fell in love with a girl

She was my everything

I pushed her away now

It's over, she's gone and I'm here

She was my first victorious defeat

And in a blink it was game over

I fell in love with a girl

She was my magical wild

Fire fulfilled all my desires

Brought me contentment when

I had none

Put a friendly noose around her throat

And now all of that is gone

She died on the outside. She

Was my second, now it's over, look at the moon

I fell in love with a girl

We went back ages

We always knew we had each other

But no one could save us

Falling in love with all the wrong things

Alex in Alaska. By Corrina Pariyar

ME

I am a free spirit. I know myself. I find happiness in people I'm close to in raves, music, traveling, FREEDOM. I can usually read people and I'm very understanding. I have strong ideas that don't waver. I don't always take the most accepted sides, like many in my family. I know and like who I am, what I represent, and what I believe in. People don't influence me, I won't be pushed into drugs, violence, or believing $2+2=5$.

I like and am proud of the way I was raised as a small child. If I adopt or take care of kids, I will do the same. I like India, and things from there since I was a little boy. I put a lot of me into people. I either have people that don't affect me and people I would give everything to and then nothingness left over.

I make good choices but don't flaunt them so they get ignored. I'm older than I am. I'm more mature than most people my age. I have been this way probably all my life.

I'm afraid of being abandoned, left, pushed away, getting hurt, being wrong about who I let in. I love animals and am empathetic. I either care or don't. It's hard for people to "get me." I hide my pain and then show it and realize both aren't good.

Life is full of irony and it is pissing me off. People who say one thing and do another are extremely bothersome because I don't know what they're doing or I should. I am an intense person. My feelings, my life, my lifestyle. The best feeling in the world is when you give someone a reason to give up and they don't. It makes you never want to let them down. The worst for me is being pushed away and people who let their priorities get in the way of their relationship with me. I'm a social salmon. I have a hard time trusting people but the people I trust would bite the bullet for me and vice versa. I judge people by their hearts not their actions.

I want to graduate high school, go to college, travel and then go to Alaska, work at Homer Brewing Company, and maybe open a restaurant. At college I want to learn how to make electronic music and maybe play at raves. Take business and culinary arts. I want to live in a small house with someone else and have a cat. I want to live close to venues for raves, good restaurants, grocery stores and a park. I want to have tea every afternoon with my good friend on our porch. I want to do school and be calm. I want to do good and make good grades. I want to be happy. I want to learn how to garden and have plants, and peppers and vegetables all at my house. I want to wake up early and eat breakfast in the park that I will live by and watch people go faster and faster. I will invite hookers and hobos over for dinner and have cake too. I will be proud of myself and only let that matter. I will do things to help others. I will be free and happy in two years.

I need my family and I will do like I do and learn from others' mistakes. I will learn and not do some of the things and the decisions they repeat. I am desperate. I am terrified of feeling bad about something that is impossible to fix. I need to be understood. I need to have access to people that do understand me.

I care a lot about others. I have dancing in my blood. I love raves, I don't care about judgments others have of me that don't know me. I think you have something to do with that. You will sport your pro-choice sticker and clothing and don't pay mind to cockroaches. I like helping people. I wait for other people to make the first move. I don't explain myself unless asked, I don't answer questions I haven't been asked. If you ever want to know anything about me, then ask. That's one things that didn't work at home: prying, snooping, tests, and therapists. Just talk to me. The last thing I wanted to say is that I never think change is impossible. People change forever, even after they die. Nothing is impossible if you try. You will hear only what you want to hear. Try hearing what you don't want to as well. It's hard to but change isn't impossible.

WHEN I'M NOT DISTRACTED

It seems that when I'm not distracted from it, I'm sad. I know I'm supposed to be OK but I'm not. I don't know how to be. I feel like all I'm doing is floating through pushing off the day I die. That's not how to live. I don't want to give up but I don't know how to be happy.

I have to be the anchor for everybody else and I'm not even strong enough for myself. It's pathetic. I've been depressed since I was 12. I don't have any meaningful relationships. I don't know how to love back. When I say "I love you" to someone, it's because I want them to feel loved. I want to love but every time it works out they disappear or die. I have a bad habit of falling head over heels for the types that can't exist.

I know I need school but now it's just too much. I want people to stop being addicted but I want to be there too. For people to stop cutting but I really want to. I'm a great planner but I can't do anything. I want to get a job but I've been getting my references and contacts for a month. I don't have the energy to get through 5 minutes. I'm a chain smoker because I'm always stressed out. I was looking for some paper because I was brainstorming my "coping skills" and writing seemed better than cutting or taking pills and sleeping my mood off.

I found this notebook, I opened it and realized I got it out of Taylor's room. It had some unfinished letters to me. I miss her so much. If I knew for sure that if I died right now, I'd be with her, I'd do it. But I think the closest I'd get to that would be in a plot which wouldn't happen being that my parents are the cremating type. I think I'm going to lay down "asleep" and pretend to sleep until it happens.

Note to self. Throw this away tomorrow.

I

if I could be

all that I need

all that I want to be

would you be there

would you believe

would you beLIEve in me

I want to love myself

as i do you

i want to be like you

i want to be free

i want to see

i want to see

everything

you mean to me

i want to be

i want to see

i want to be me

THE BLACK SKY

The black sky, the empty lies.

Your maliciousness, my awkward viciousness.

The brokenness fills me with hopelessness.

Tear me apart with your scarred hands.

My soul walking across the desert lands.

All fucked up and ready to die.

You hurt me to a place where

I hopelessly cry. My heart is all dried up while I'm

all tied up.

Never enough

Never enough

Everything's dead.

Yet, everyone says it's all in my head.

Take it out on me.

Force me to see the making of fakeness,

The empty wonderful greatness.

I'm still waiting and I'm still waiting on you.

ALL MINE

you be my reason to stay alive

as fake as a Gucci model

ill be my reason to die

as real as a bleeding wound

pick me up, tell me a lie

as much pain as I can take

at least all the pain as I keep

it is all mine

im as fake as a christmas card

im all that you want

im the life that's not so hard

shes so blind

from the cuts on my arm

to my aunts farm

she sees absolutely nothing

except the things that I am not

I am my own problems

The victim on the floor

I am my own trap

I am my own whore

Ive seen the crippled dance

Ive seen her kill with just one glance

She brought me back with just one dance

Im as fake as silicone

Im as fake as my mothers home

Im as fake as my conversations on the phone

and I want someone to share this with

and I want to be less victimized

i want to ruin myself

i want to open my eyes

i always hurt myself

i make people hate me

when Im all tied up I feel free

take my hand, taste my blood

take a breath and weep with me

sitting on my bathroom floor

crying like some beat up whore

need to get up walk out the door

need to put back on that smile

so there will be something more

today in the bathtub I fantasized

i sat there thinking about suicide

im willing to live

im willing to die

i thought about slitting my wrists

holding the razor tight in my fist

you think it would be odd

finding me in a tub me and a bottle of suave

if it werent me I would laugh

like i already do to mask

bleeding like a paint stroke

take a pill

swallow my tongue

began to choke

too stressed to bleed

need a cigarette to smoke

I quit cutting Sunday

now im choking on my feelings

it was the only thing I had left to take away

just a negative of a thesis that wanted to be loved

FAKE

this is the way I want to go

with everyone knowing

i want it to be slow

i want to feel it all

come out of me light as a feather

as painless and free

suicide is painless

suicide is free

suicide is everything

suicide is for me

AUD

you are the perfect drug

the perfect touch

the perfect human

the most immaculate

beauty you can touch in

this reality

the most complete feeling that makes you

weep at its very presence

this is the primal identity

you are my primal source

you caress me with your being

you love me

Huka
3
tha
Boom
Boom

Arabian
Knights
in tha south

ENTIER

i want to smash a mirror with my bare fist
i want to ride a camel through times square
i want to get a tattoo
i want to shave off my hair
i want to run naked in the rain
i want to live simple and plain
i want to fill up
never come down
want to run away
want to leave town
want to scream without making a sound
i want to find treasure
and tell all the people what i found
i want to be ok with myself
never ask for help
i want to be everything I never was
i want to run away and come back
just because
want to slap the shit out of a few people
get em back

i want to apologize

to everyone ive hurt

even if im not on a 12 step system

i want them to talk

i want to listen

I want to break all my ties

run away forever

open up my mind

i want to call 911

just to say what's up

want to drink

some nyquil straight out of a cup

wanna smoke out with my aunt

pierce my nipples

wanna throw a pebble in a lake

and watch how it ripples

i want to sail a sail boat

into the abysses

want to be covered in 19000 kisses

all from you

BAKED

today

I played in a sprinkler

then filled this big dirt-filled hole

of mud and water and

it was so dirty

i realized that you have to be true to yourself

and be comfortable

to be comfortable

is better than all the sex drugs and rock and roll

in the universe

i realize that i may not always be what people

want me to be

i can't change to fit the mood of others

and i can't fight urges i get to play around

or do stupid shit

because that is what makes me feel complete

and you know no matter how hard i try to be

someone else's wet dream of a human being

i'm always going to end up being stupid broken

silly fucked up

muddy little me

In fireweed, Homer, Alaska.

ENLIGHTENMENT

empty slate

perfect state

everything is beautiful

cloud nine

its not too late

FREE AS A BIRD

I'm as free as a bird
As gorgeous as a gospel choir
I will not stand for your
Negativity I have learned not
To believe in liars. All they
Can do is make you feel
Good for a while until you
Are free. I think you have to
Realize you are human and
You have to witness your
Self bleed. You have to
Realize that you are
Only human and humans
Have needs don't be afraid
To let go and dive
Right in. Your soul is the
Only thing that leads.

THE OTHER HALF

the most beautiful thing I have ever held on to

has been down sized

and laughed at

i have nothing to show

besides a headache

a buddha

and fucking wonderful memories

it was better than

jesus on his knees doin the dirty dirty

but fuck it

i need a fix

I cant help it that i cling to strangers

and betray the ones I love

i dont know why I give my being away

to people who dont care a fraction

about me as I do them

i dont understand why i cling so much

am i that incomplete?

its really sad

to cry over someone you knew for 10 hours

or to cut over a therapists chuckle

or to want to kill yourself because

someone got a fucking cupcake with more

sprinkles than you

what the fuck?

this is me

i live

i want

i crave

i cling

i need

i cry

i hurt

i drink

i believe that every breath that comes out of my

mouth

is either profound

or shit

because that is how it is to be me

if someone doesnt call you

and you know a party

that they probably will be at

hours away

and you run away

just to see them as they walk in

because then something might be fixed

you are me

and you are

fucking pathetic

just like me

this isnt one of those youre good

find your pain and cope,

7 habits of highly effective teens,

you mean something,

bull shit

this is me

as most of you know

or don't

i have found a perfect escape

and all everyone wants

to do is bring me down

im sure this

will not relate to my life

at all

within the next 48 hours

but until then i feel shitty

and I feel like

complaining

and venting

and I feel better now

you know when people

get ruined

they turn around and ruin people

that don't deserve it

i am the type of person

who does that kind of ruthless shit

this is only ½

of the picture

I don't write when I'm the other

half

CANDY

i have found something

new

wondrous perfection

it's like I'm running away

with the most beautiful decision

to a place I once knew before

this is what I want my life to be like

i am so glad I don't have all the things anymore

free of guilt

free of shame

i'm overall clean

never again

YELLOW

some things we break

we cannot fix

being wounded

is something I don't miss

i am doing wonderfully

i haven't cried in a while

haven't cut in 2 weeks

today i cracked a smile

its not that im always

sad or broken or used

its just that way when i get

around you

the first time in a week

it was only a flash

my stomach tightened up

my skin ached for a gash

i wanted to die and take you too

but wouldn't that be my style

i am so untrue

if I die before you do

ill go to heaven and wait for you...

Pat and Nathan

Do not go crazy over this. I know it's probably a huge test of keeping it together for Mom. I have not just disappeared or been kidnapped or killed by some maniac. Remember I am not just some four year old. I can wash clothes and cook and navigate international airports. Remember the talk. I have left until Sunday (most likely late tonight) when I will be home. I have an ID with me. I have someone number with me that is 15 minutes away from me and another that is 45 (both are relatives) I'm going to be fine. This is not a rebellious thing. It is me knowing what's right for me better than you can grasp. Remember why I had a big smile on my face on Wednesday? This is why.

Love
Alex

PS don't trip out and report me as a runaway and not do the shot clinic and make everything come to a halt this isn't as big of a deal as you think it is.

PPS it will be OK, I can take care of myself.

PPPS I'm sleeping over at Bub's house

I PROMISE

candy coated glitter blisses

and glowing sparkly trickle kisses

its like a wonderful sign from god

that everythings going to be alright

everythings going to fit

it will all be perfect

even if just for tonight

who would have known that it would turn this

way

i got it all

im winning

this is where I want to stay

i have a number and some money and an email

address

this is all I want and need

not a thing more

not a thing less

this is who I want to be

i feel light

i feel wanted

i feel free

i feel loved

and cared for

and I feel like this is the perfect me

glow sticks and music

beautiful strangers

and im driven in their car

i couldnt be more pleased

untie all my knots

MERRY CHRISTMAS

It bubbles

It clouds

We tend to laugh aloud

Shotguns

And south park

A wonderful

Warmth

Coated in bliss

A Christmas

A kiss

A time to

Give and take

A time to forget

Why cant we be Jewish

All they have to get out of the attic is

A candle holder

We have fucking boxes on boxes

Of boxes of shit

With hangy things

And lights

And piglet

And pooh and eeyore

And merry and winkle

And gods and goddesses

That toy and sprinkles

And snow and blow

My cares away in a world of Kenny G

And Bjork and beans

And meaningless everythings

Merry Christmas to all especially audra cause she

needs it

A

Love everyone to death

E

X

Hate me

alex

WELCOME TO MY INNER LIGHT

i havent cut since last september.
im feeling kinda down,
i need crutches and oxygen tanks
and my godly crown
and sit me on my sickly throne
and i can see through your windows
i cant stand the rain
you dont feel loneliness
the way that I do
"taking a few years off my life"
is good because they take your last ones first.
so i would rather live up my life while everything is
extreme
and fuck all your cubicles and fuck all your dress
appropriately
signs and shit... i'm going to be a writer (poet) and
a brewery owner and im beyond positive
i will be smoking my home grown marijuana in the
days with
my morbidly obese beasts (aka) cats mountaineering
a

gelatinous furry climb to the top of my face at 12am
(the time I wake up every day I go to work) and they
shall lick my face and hair and any orifices that may
be
exposed to their wrath. so when I am on cloud nine
with
my two cats (the morbidly obese poodle eaters) we
will listen to bjork as we read and watch the sun
go down over the beach (that I can walk to)
the two volcanoes that are in the ocean but if youre
a good
swimmer im sure you could ... so while you realize
that
nothing shall ever come about in everyones life mine
will be different and profound. I welcome you to
bask in my
inner light.
im probably going to get pissed off so much that I just
hang myself with your garments that you left
with me.

HOMELESS AND HOMESICK

my sky

is only glowing

for a moment

or two

until the sky comes

crashing down

with jagged

pieces ripping into you

finding pointless

memories

for a reason to be strong

knowing in your heart

that you

will never

find the place

where you finally

belong

.

FROZEN

cold blood

crowding your veins

pushing and shoving

trying to escape

eaten by the heart

raped by the brain

there comes a time

when things can not

be saved

all I know is I'm lonely

and I miss everything

and all my nights are sleepless

and it all remains the same

snuggle up

you're not alone

you're just a little wounded

without a home

BROKEN HANDS

rolling over to a porcelain sunrise

and plastic tears you will never realize

everything gone wrong in a world so true

and the only lie left is a lie like you

WHAT DO YOU WANT TO DO BEFORE YOU DIE?

Go to Europe

Go hunting

Meet Bjork

Slap the shit out of a few individuals

Own a brewery

Get famous

Get a tit job

Call everyone I have ever hurt and apologize

Smoke pot with my art teacher

Have sex with someone I don't know the first name
of

Fly in a hot air balloon

Adopt a hobo

I'm sure there's more but I'm tired.

What do you want to do before you die?

VISIONS OF THE FUTURE

Alex with his aunt, Karen Berger, and uncle,
Steve McCasland.

I would be interested in brewing because my aunt owns a brewery in Homer Alaska and I go there to visit every summer and Christmas. When they retire they are leaving the brewery to me.

I think photography would be fascinating to me because I would be able to travel and go to events and parties. I think taking pictures, traveling, and getting into interesting places for a paycheck is the thing for me.

I would like to travel to the UK because it is modern in an old classical way. I also really like English accents so I would probably just listen to people.

I find chemistry fascinating because it breaks down simple process and action and makes them complex. It's so analytical that it makes simple things exotic.

Art is intriguing to me because art is a form of communication that visually explains what words cannot. I think art makes talking quiet.

I think Iceland is interesting because it's a big, peaceful, friendly nation. They don't have their own army, they have never been in a war, and they were the first country to elect a woman as president.

India is also very beautiful place. It is full of euphoric history and culture even though now it is consumed with violence and poverty and child labor to make silk for Pottery Barn.

Being a writer would be nice because you could do a lot of research on whatever subject fills your twinky.

I also think that to have the capability to organize your thoughts enough to write a 300 page book is something to brag all about.

I have taken a class at MCC on oil painting and it was lovely to me how you could mix the rich colors and fade them.

SELECTIONS
from 2003-2004

＝＝

16 – 18 YEARS OLD
Lone Star Expeditions, East Texas
Mount Bachelor Academy, Oregon
San Marcos Treatment Center, Texas

Mount Bachelor Academy, Oregon, 2003.

REFLECTIONS

Skiing, Mount Bachelor, Oregon, 2004.

BY JAMIE PIERCE-FANGMAN
Registrar at Mount Bachelor Academy, Oregon

When I think back on the times I spent with Alex, I am reminded that he was an old soul, insightful beyond his years. Alex was a kind, compassionate young man. He also struggled with his personal demons on darker days. He and his mother, Pat, became family. I loved the times we spent together, the meals we shared whether in Oregon or in Texas. Back at Mount Bachelor Academy, I had a memorial garden for the sweet souls like Alex who found this world too much to bear, each represented by a butterfly. Alex's was yellow. The stone in the garden surrounded by flowers read, "When someone you love becomes a memory, the memory becomes a treasure." A treasure he was and always will be in my heart.

BY DAVID REED

Alex's therapist at San Marcos Treatment Center

I had the pleasure of getting to know Alex as his therapist while he was in treatment at a residential treatment center. I saw Alex in both individual and family therapy. After leaving our program, he transitioned to a longer-term therapeutic program. Alex got along well with his peers. He was a kind and sensitive young man, very attuned to the feelings of others. He was blessed with four remarkable parents who cared about him a great deal. As a group they came for family therapy each week, and if they had differences or conflicts, they put them aside so that they could best support Alex. Although it has been many years since I had been with Alex, I remember his easy and kind way as if he were here with us yesterday.

Richard, Alex, Pat, and Jason
in front of Alex's dorm at Mt. Bachelor, Oregon.

BY RICHARD WARE

A letter to Alex from his dad when he was at Mount Bachelor Academy in Oregon.

Richard with Alex.

Dear Alex,

I am writing this letter to let you know how I feel about the way you have been acting and why you are at M.B.A. You are old enough to realize that missing school, smoking grass, staying up all night, and being rude and disrespectful are not to be tolerated by your parents.

It has been one month since you started Mount Bachelor Academy. You can graduate from high school in the next thirteen months if you will stay on track. You have a great opportunity to make new friends and study hard. Take a good look at yourself and decide what direction you would like to take in life.

The last year has brought everything to a head. You were going downhill fast. Attitude, lack of communication, missing classes, and disrespect towards both your mom and myself. I was mad and hurt that the more we tried to understand and help, the more you pushed us away and treated us as if we were stupid. I try to treat you as if you were intelligent, articulate and gifted. I did not talk down to you and expected you to treat me the same.

Towards the end, fear for your health and safety, worry about bad decisions you were making, and your choice of friends had me awake at night thinking, "Where did I go wrong?"

As you mature I hope for you to make good choices, show love and respect for your family and friends, set goals and achieve them, and look at life as an opportunity to help others.

I feel bad that I wasn't a better parent. I was not strong enough to guide you in a better direction. I do feel you are in the right place and hope that you will take advantage of everything M. B. A. has to offer.

You are no longer a little boy but a young man, and I am looking forward to us talking man to man. Maturity also brings responsibility for yourself and your actions.

You will always have my unconditional love.

Love,

Dad

SCHOOL ASSIGNMENTS

Mount Bachelor Academy, 2004.

HIGH EXPECTATIONS –
THE GREAT SEARCH FOR
SOMETHING THAT WASN'T THERE

CHAPTER ONE

There was once a nest and in this nest there was one egg with four big birds. They let it hatch and fed it worms and raised it like it should be. One day the fuzzy little baby bird flapped his wings and knocked all the other birds down. They got up and said, "It's time for you to leave. The baby bird begged and pleaded."

They saw a hole with moles in it right under their nest. They said they look happy and well. They said those baby moles are doing just as they should. I too want my baby to do this. They will show him how to be, yes, and it will work. So they pushed the baby bird right out of that nest and its little body not capable of flight fell into the hole that his parents thought to be the answer.

He, a bit puzzled and bruised, looked into the eyes of the mole and said, "What am I doing here?"

He replied simply, "Your parents love you and I will show you how to be. First Rule you are now a mole. You are not to open your wings for you are different than us and that is what is wrong. Second Rule is that you shall trust me and do just as I say. I am always right and you will always be wrong without me. Third rule, you can no longer be with your parents. They are too far up in the tree to see but they are there and they love you. Go now and sleep. I will teach you in the morning."

And with that the baby bird that was used to grass and feathers settled on a bed of rocks and dirt and fell into a deep sleep with his head in a puddle of mud he created with his tears.

CHAPTER TWO

The next day the bird woke up and over him sat a fat mole with long teeth and huge claws. He came to him and said, "When we are awake we dig because moles dig and we are moles. Come here, come with me. I'll show you what to do."

He waddled down a corridor of dirt and said, "Here, let me show you." With that, the mole dug ferociously with his massive claws. The little bird tried to concentrate, but through the hail of dirt and the occasional earthworm being flung in his general direction, it was quite a task. The mole stopped after a minute or so and looked hopefully into the bird's little eyes and said, "Your turn."

The bird walked hesitantly to the spot where the mole had been standing in moments earlier and with a confused look started wobbly picking and scratching with his beak and claws. Miserable bits of dirt and dust came off and ended up cutting the bird's little claws. The mole looked on with disapproval and disappointment. He said, "Stop! Stop! What's wrong with you? I have thirteen kids and they all dig. They are all happy. My wife and I dig and we all dig great. We are moles and we dig. You are a mole. Now dig!"

The little bird looked at him and wondered how he could turn into a mole that everyone wanted him to be. He went on pecking mouth beakfuls of dirt and moving, but at the end of the day after using all of his energy, he stood in the same place he had in the morning and looked at the same wall of dirt that was there earlier. Nothing had changed. The mole groaned and said, "He will learn. Because we are moles and moles dig." The little bird, dirty and worn from the work and rocks tearing at him in his quest to be a mole. He had experienced what he had to do and realized that they wouldn't love him until he did it.

CHAPTER THREE

Months of this process continued. He started comparing himself to the other moles that were being compared to him. He was growing feathers where his fuzz once was but he dared not to break rule one for he was a constant disappointment and tried not to worsen it.

After going back and forth day after day, the mole said to the bird, "You are different, very different. You are a failure. You cannot dig and you don't look like everyone else. What am I going to do? You won't ever be enough, and if you ever are I will want more so that you can never achieve your goal."

CHAPTER FOUR

One day, by the water, the bird was thinking to himself. He remembered his family and he remembered his dormant wings. He remembered that before he was a mole, he was a bird. He remembered stretching his wings and wishing his parents had taught him how to fly. He remembered that with the best intentions and with love they threw him into the moles' hole below their nest. They looked really nice from above. They worked well and did what they needed to. They were perfect and did what they were made to do. He went back to the hole and walked right back into it.

CHAPTER FIVE

One day the mole said, "I have grown tired of this. You aren't welcome here anymore. Leave tomorrow morning." This came as an unexpected shock to the bird. He walked out of the hole the next morning and glared into the sun until the whites turned to black and he couldn't see for a few minutes. He walked through the grass and stopped at the water hole.

He said to himself, "Moles are moles and moles dig." He then thought to himself about being a bird all along and his thought the day before. He then thought, birds are birds and birds fly. He felt a great hope and happiness he had not felt since he had been in his nest.

POETRY, NOTES, & DRAWINGS

Sitting in the rafters at Lone Star Expeditions,
East Texas, July 2003

PONDER THE STARS, AVOID THE EGG SHELLS

Ponder the stars, avoid the egg shells

Hope for the best, receive otherwise

Try to stay out of the way

Attempt to exhaustion the unachievable

Chewing constantly more than was bitten

Experiencing more that can ever be written

Trace the clues, drop the crumbs

Remember where my hope comes from

Separate essence from illusion

Seeking our creator

March 18, 2004: Alex with his dad, Richard, his "Bubba" Jason, and his mom, Pat, on top of Mount Bachelor in Oregon on Alex's 17th birthday.

MEANING OF LIFE

Meaning of life is
To find balance
In a cycle of
Suffering and healing
BE CONTENT
BE PARADOX

GO WITH THE FLOW

If we go with

the flow of the

river we will get

to the ocean

we will also get

there if we take

a row boat up

stream to the

ocean

The first will

arrive naturally with

ease

the second will

work intensely and

arrive meeting the same goal

who will appreciate it more?

so which was better?

BEING IN "CONTROL"

Being in "control"
of an opened mind and
being in control of
a body are quite
different.
Being able to move
freely within one's
psyche.
You are in control
of your mind
when you surrender that
control and allow
your mind to wander
freely and with purpose
of having no destination.

ALWAYS HUNGRY FOR THE WRONG THINGS

Sorry this will never be
what you ordered send
it back to the kitchen
throw it away
order something new
taste and cringe
never enough
not perfect enough
send it back
sweating chefs
behind knives just
trying to be alright
what's the special today?
it's too strong, it's too spicy
it's too foreign, it's sour
spit it out before you chew
it up. It's too raw
cook it to oblivion
this cannot fit

RANDOM OBSERVATIONS
OF LIFE

- A persistent flow of H2O can crumble the hardiest of stone. Strength is weaker than persistent weakness against the strong. Cast a stone into a body of water, splash a stone wall with a wave. Power, strength and force are futile against enduring gentleness.

- We limit ourselves by fear. There is no such thing as permanence. There is no reason to limit conscious expansion because of fear of getting "stuck" there. An optical illusion that baffles us into a state of realities the "that can't be, but is now and isn't going away oh shit" problem that can arise from time to time and even though fear, in its animalistic, instinctiveness, kneejerk perception, feels exactly as real as it can be. It remains to not be. Everything you can get in to, you can equally get out of.

- Anger and fear are the most motivating emotions because they are the most uncomfortable to stay with.

Alex with friends and family at his
high school graduation party, 2004.
First row: Jill Wimberly, K'lee Ware, Kyle, Viki Linthicum,
Bailey Linthicum, Penny Maloy Gifford, Molly Maloy.
Second row: Fernando Rogers, Becky Warren,
Pat Stone, Nathan Stone, Alex Ware, Amy Ware,
Libby Langford, Kay Bailey, Randy Merrill.
Third Row: Richard Ware, Roxanne Ware,
Salem McKenna Ware, Jason Ware.

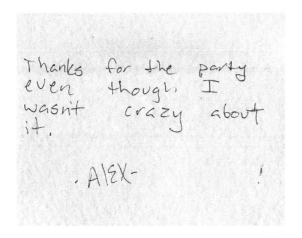

Thanks for the party even though I wasn't crazy about it.

. ALEX-

SELECTIONS
from 2004 – 2006

18 – 19 YEARS OLD
McLennan Community College,
Waco, Texas

Alex in New Braunfels, Easter, 2006.

REFLECTIONS

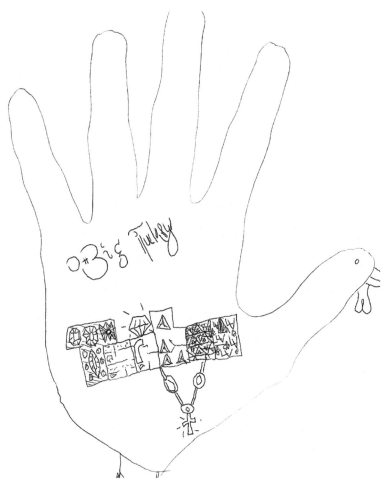

Some friends referred to Alex
by his nickname, "Turk," short for "Turkey."

BY EMILY WARREN

Alex's friend in Waco, Texas

I feel deeply conflicted on what exactly to write. I considered Alex so many different things. Thinking of him and the memories I have of him bring me back to a time in my life that was very confusing, chaotic, toxic, free, wild, dark. SO many different things swell inside me. We were teenagers and we were wild. We wanted to show our independence and defy our parents and be (completely misguided and misunderstood teenagers.) We were young and dumb. In a nutshell, we were idiots. I don't know if Alex would want me to share all the dirty, grimy things we tend to never tell our parents.

At the same time. I feel that when we pass on, we are able to look at life completely haze-free. We understand all that we thought that mattered actually does not. Life would seem so much clearer after the fact. I think that even though teenage Alex (young, wild, and eclectic) would never want his parents to know all the crazy, that after leaving us he would be OK with you knowing if it brought you peace.

Was all of it crazy?! No. But all of it is kind of frowned upon in the general law-abiding society, and I feel slightly ashamed for saying I would do it all over again in a heartbeat. I wouldn't change an of it. It was the best-worst time of my life. Alex was part of that.

I want to share the Alex I know . . . I was thinking about how to write this. I am not sure the best way to describe the Alex that I knew. Thinking of the memories I had with him causes a rush of different emotions. I'm not sure who Alex was really. I saw glimpses of him. I saw different parts of his personality a little at a time. Some of the sides I saw of him really touched me and has made a permanent etch on my soul. Other parts of him were scary. He was a guy with so many different faces. But they all equally defined who he was.

The first time I met Alex he introduced himself as "Turk," short for Turkey. He was this skinny, knees-and-elbows, lanky kid. His clothes were two sizes too large. When he spoke he sounded like he had an accent but not a southern one you might expect from a kid in Texas. It was a drawling urban upper crust. It was uniquely Turk. I am pretty sure I met him through Jack and Jill (Jill and Justin) at their tiny nothing of an apartment by Texas State Technical College. I don't think I thought very much ᶜ him the first time we met. He was kind of an ͏l, skinny thing. He was very funny though, and ͗nk that's what really kind of drew me towards his sense of humor. He was quick-witted and ͏ass. He would make jokes not everyone in the would get. He was odd and he knew it, but ͏ᵉ it well.

Shandi and Alex were always together. There was never one without the other. When they were separated you could tell the other one lost a bit of themselves without their counterpart and would become more of a wall flower than the center of the party. Together they complemented one another's personality. The room and party would always tend to gather around them. I wanted to hang around them too. I wanted to know these crazy cartoon-personality people. They were demanding of attention and I was more than willing to give it, to hear what outrageous and off the wall topic they would converse about.

Turk and Shandi's apartment wasn't far and I would go over there after work to hang out. Turk and Shandi were the people you went to if you wanted to get anything. They were also one of the very few of us, at the time, that had an apartment of their own.

Turk had a closet in their bedroom that he had turned into a smoke shack. It had white shag carpet and a Jimi Hendrix Indian art Poster that hung on one of the walls with a black light above it. He had stuck glow in the dark stars to the ceiling. Us three would lay on the shag carpet and pass fat blunts back and forth, staring at that Jimi Hendrix poster. Sometimes we would get stuck on religion or some current world event that was happening at the time (none of which I can recall) and stay in that closet for endless hours, cheefing away.

Turk would find these crazy songs and I have no idea where he got ahold of them or how to look them up. He would play music for us to listen to while we sat/laid and talked as we smoked the day/night away. That closet was like a cocoon from the outside. The apartment was the shell we could retreat to from the outside world. The closet closed off the shell sealing us shut from everything and everyone. It was a safe place. I have such vivid memories of us laying and talking about nothing, being in our own world and bubble and at the same time I can't recall a single thing we spoke about but I remember that feeling of feeling safe, feeling hidden with them.

Almost always Alex was a counterpart to some new drug adventure we would take together. Without him I don't think I would have half of those crazy twenty-something life experiences you're not supposed to talk about. He influenced me in so many different ways when it came to exploring this new strange world with my eyes and mind wide open. He had a way of making something completely insane sound reasonable. I can't help but smile when I think about how passionate he would be about feeling and being part of the world you live in. At the same time I wasn't able to truly appreciate those words till now. There are so many things he said that were lost in the mind of a drug-induced twenty-year-old but vibrate the walls of my entire being now. Older, wiser, and much less of an idiot. I miss him.

Alex was always trying to save the world. Maybe he wasn't trying to save the world—just better us. He would try to convince us that being a vegetarian was a much better choice. More than once he would put on some brutal PETA campaign video showing mutilated and caged animals while we were completely stoned out of our minds. Not cool. He would also preach these PETA facts to us while eating macaroni at Bush's Chicken while the rest of us ate chicken strips. I thought that was funny.

He got this video once, "How to not get arrested," a step-by step-guide of what to and what not to say to the police when you have paraphernalia or drugs on you. Interesting and educational. He would have us watch videos about world beliefs and the power of positive thinking. "What the Bleep do you know" was actually a pretty good movie even though I was completely against it and rolled my eyes at him. He would play Bob Marley and preach. He convinced me that *Absolutely Fabulous* was the greatest show ever made and we watched the show in its entirety from first season to last.

There was a lot of dark. There was some anger. Some things that drug addicts tend to do. Steal and lie. Then justify those actions without reason. We all had those moments then. We were all struggling with addiction. He would scare me with the amount of intake of his leisure. Then we would all laugh about it afterwards. Life momentarily and in small paragraphs was a joke and sometimes not real at all. What made our group of misfits was that each of us had our own inner demons. I never knew his and he never knew mine. But we each knew there was pain and we just accepted it and welcomed each other into our messy way of navigating through it. It was a black mark in my life, living that way. But knowing Alex made the insane bearable and acceptable. He held my hand without ever knowing he did. At the end of my own journey, I felt like I never really knew the real him. I don't know how else to say that.

BY AMBER GIRNUS
Alex's friend in Waco, TX

Alex was one of the most unique individuals I ever met. He truly was an individual. He was constantly drawing insane, psychedelic, thought-provoking (sometimes sarcastically funny) images that will be etched in my memory forever. I met Alex for the first time at Miss Nellie's Pretty Place in Cameron Park. It was my first time to take LSD and my mind was at a loss on how to "let go." Everyone was enjoying themselves, but I was so stuck in my ego brain that there was no escaping from this drab reality.

Alex and Shandi were sitting at the fountain, literally quoting and acting out various parts from Disney's *Alice in Wonderland*. It was so surreal, his voice and accent for each character were so spot-on that it was as if the movie had come alive right before my very eyes. After this specific moment, I started letting go. This was the summer of 2005, and it was actually pretty mild.

I distinctly remember Alex pointing out the sign that said, "Wildflowers in Progress," and how appropriate it was for our minds and the occasion. We were total "wildflowers progressing," making connections on such parallel levels of existence. When he ran out of 'rock-chalk' in which to enhance the concrete, walls and benches, he then turned to using the resin from various joint roaches that were saved in his car. Just mix a little saliva, and voila! It was the Alex way, of course!

One also can't help but remember the time he dropped LSD and drove out of town to some rave. For some reason or another, he took all the tobacco out of his cigarettes and re-rolled it with joint papers. There was always copious amounts of marijuana around this kid. Always. Shortly after ditching town, he was riding in the car with Shandi, toking up the ganja, acid kicking in, and—sure enough—got pulled over by a cop. The cop could smell the marijuana before he got out of his cruiser so naturally asked them to step out to search the vehicle. LSD Brain, incoming! While the cop rummaged through the vehicle, desperately trying to find the source of this pungent odor, Alex and Shandi made shadow puppets with the flashing lights of the police car and giggled and laughed hysterically until they couldn't breathe. It must have been a scene for the books. The cop got increasingly angry, as he matter-of-factly pulled out the case of rolled cigarettes.

"AHA!" he exclaimed. "Do you want to explain what this is?"

"Those are my cigarettes!" said Alex.

The officer broke open all the "joints" in hopes to charge these kiddos with reckless youth hood, to no avail. He ended up letting them go and never found out why they were acting so out of this world or where the marijuana came from. I got to hear this tale a few hours after the incident when he called me from a payphone deep in the ghetto, lost and tripping his face off. It was amazing.

An Alex quirk that stands out was his split personality. One minute, he was a homosexual raver; the next, a disenfranchised African American woman. His personality stretched over different aspects of human nature in which those particular groups of people may not have had it as privileged as he. It was as if he convinced himself he actually was the person he was fighting for. His passion for being a humanitarian ran so deep, it was truly torturous for his spirit to live in such a misguided and confused world.

My first taste of vegetarianism came from our friendship. I grew up with a strict, poor Southern diet of red meat and potatoes. Anything else wasn't human. Alex didn't talk much about the horrors of animal consumption, but he definitely led silently by example. I happened upon a PETA DVD in his apartment one day and asked to borrow it. He seemed pleased by the fact that someone would try to understand the horrors of this overpopulated, gluttonous world. This was super effective in changing the way I perceived food as a whole, and not a day goes by that my meat intake doesn't have some form of guilt attached. I struggle with this dichotomy to this very day.

My favorite anti-animal paraphernalia was a magnet on his refrigerator that showed a silhouetted chicken and the words "I am NOT a nugget".

It's very heartening to know my friend was at the forefront of such thinking, especially before it was mainstream or even considered socially acceptable. I was told he made a conscious decision to not eat animals at the age of three. Conscious, indeed.

I never had sleepovers with friends, especially in adulthood. Something about the vulnerability of the whole thing scared me away. But we had sleepovers at Alex's every weekend and vice versa. We would stay up all night discussing patterns and mysteries of the universe, drawing, writing, listening to music. Paranormal shenanigans were always on the menu as well.

One night we had taken MDMA and had a super fun bonding session with some friends. We made a pact that whoever died first would have to come back and haunt the others. It was a pinky promise, so it had to be done. One night about a week after Alex passed, he actually appeared before me while I was in the bathroom.

At this very moment, at 3 a.m. on the dot, my phone rang. It was his best friend, Shandi, crying and saying she was listening to his favorite Moby song. I knew then just how surreal and amazing this life can be, no matter how much it hurts when the people you love are gone. Perhaps our thought energies all collided in the exact moment to create an apparition of him. Maybe he actually wanted to say hello and was making sure to haunt me since, ya know, it was a blood pact. Maybe we are all delusional and life is full of meaningless coincidences.

I choose to believe in love, life, and the power of our thoughts. Sometimes I'm guilty of straying from this mantra, but it brings comfort in such a dark world. Perhaps we reincarnate and get another chance to play out our lives exactly how we want them. Alex actually introduced me to the Buddhist philosophy. It struck a deep chord within, being a realistic approach to human nature and beyond.

These moments of adolescence and young adulthood literally created the person I am today. I am so grateful I had someone with whom I could relate on a deep human level. If there's one thing he taught me in this life: it is to love one another, no matter what. Do not pass judgement on others; their circumstances differ from mine and yours. Be kind to strangers; it will make you feel better, and you may be the only person who has ever smiled at them and offered a helping hand. We all know these things, but how often we forget on a daily basis, be it from frustration, stress, or the routine of mundane life.

Everyone loved Alex, even if he annoyed them or if they didn't understand that "crazy ass white boy." I think he taught us a little something about our shadow selves, and that's why he was loved by all. It's been a pleasure and an honor to call him my friend, and it has made me happy reminiscing on his wacky self! There was never a dull moment. He kept us all entertained, thinking, listening, loving, forgiving. What a bright star to still shine so bright in our hearts. From this realm to the next . . . !

SCHOOL ASSIGNMENTS

Flying high on the trampoline that had been
part of the family since he was four years old.

GEORGE ORWELL

"Until they become conscious they will never rebel, and until after they have rebelled they cannot become conscious."

— George Orwell, *1984*

Orwellian; relating to the work of the British novelist George Orwell (1903-1950), especially the totalitarian state depicted in *1984*. When a person's name becomes an adjective it may be concluded that their person has made quite a mark on their world. These would include Freudian, Sadistic, and Kafkaesque. This is a look into the man who gave meaning to the notion of Orwellian.

Born Eric Blair, the man we have come to know as George Orwell was a prisoner of his class, in the jail of a sugar coated British caste system. He was born into a member of the "lower-upper middle class." He grew up in an unconventional way and kept with that game plan the rest of his life. He spoke the truth on the level of common man and put down truth on paper in palatable form.

George Orwell was born in 1903 in a small village in India. His mother and father were English and worked for the empire there. His mother was 18 when he was born. His father worked as an agent for The Department of the Indian Civil Service. Even though they were not financially well off they made it by with the aid of the British Empire which they helped administer.

His family moved back to England where he went through the private school system, quite unsuccessfully. His father continued to live and work in India until he retired a few years later and came over to England with the rest of his family.

He started private school in England when he was 8. Although his family didn't have enough money to send him there, they scraped along just enough using the scholarships that he received. He was less than enthusiastic with his studies though. He neglected the whole of his school because he already had a strong direction that he couldn't be nurtured at his school.

He wanted to be a writer so he believed that he should be well-read. Since most of the students were illiterate or under literate most schools didn't stress literature as much as George Orwell would have liked. Because he put his formal education on the back burner, he got low marks and didn't go to college.

George Orwell moved back to India when he finished school to join the Burma Police Force. This is probably where his early political views originated. He quit after seeing he was supporting the

Imperialism as well as the one dominating another mentality that he wholeheartedly stood against.

He saw the poor as victims of injustice, and he still had a burned-in mentality of repulsion for them. So in a George Orwell manner he packed up and moved to the hub of the impoverished. From all of these experiences Orwell wrote his documentary *Down and Out in Paris and London*. The published edition was entitled *Burmese Days*.

Burmese Days, his first book, was published in 1934. In 1935 he came out with *A Clergyman's Daughter*, a story of a woman who has her faith changed when she is exposed to poverty, joblessness, hunger, and death.

His next book published in 1936, *Keep the Aspidistra Flying*, an account of a man who lives in poverty following his own ideals only to dampen his once bright spirit in the process.

Road to Wigan Pier is the outline of the society that he was in. It irritated his publishers because it appeared to be an attack on their lifestyle by poking fun at middle class apathy and failed government policies that would make the country more socialistic.

Homage to Catalonia was a first-hand account of the Spanish Civil War that he fought in as a rebel.

Coming Up for Air is the story of one man's contempt for modern living and his journey to go back to his roots by going to his family's farm where he grew up.

Orwell wrote his two most famous works under the influence of World War II. *Animal Farm*, a metaphorical story depicting a corrupt political regime, and *Nineteen Eighty-four*, a depiction of a totalitarian ruled state and the struggle of the one free spirit that had to go through it. This was the work in which the word Orwellian emerged.

George Orwell is one of my favorite writers because he knows how to take a heavy subject and get it across to the general public. Since the average person isn't going to read about political theory, you can raise the consciousness of a society if you speak the language. I think that is Orwell's strength. He can speak the truth while speaking the language. That was the powerful impact with *Animal Farm* because it expressed his political theory for the common man.

I also have respect that he gambled by not always doing the socially accepted by following his own ideals and beliefs. He also wasn't afraid of pissing people off. This is admirable because most authors are more concerned with how many copies they sell as opposed to staying with what they believe. George Orwell was different in that he had the courage to speak truth to power. By saying the truth he stayed true to himself.

I also respect his idea on authority and how too much can and will lead to oppression, corruption, and eventually anarchy.

No wonder George Orwell has the distinction of being known as an icon of anti-authoritarianism.

HARD DECISION

Looking up, there are people scrambling around trying to find a seat on a lifeboat. At this point I could stay in my seat or give it to a stranger.

I choose to stay where I am. In a perfect scenario all the "lifers" would get the boats and the coalition of the willing to die would get to wait on deck for the ocean. My first response was to give up my seat to the first person who came by. But after some thought I decided to stay put and this is why.

If I was to give up my seat I would want someone who was going to take advantage of this chance to change. I couldn't very well administer personality tests and review applications. I would rather live with certainty that I would help change this world, than die with the uncertainty that the stranger I just gave my life to would. I would take the experience and do all that I could when got back to safety to help, be selfless, charitable, and honorable. I can insure what my future actions will be, to insure what the future actions of a complete stranger I'm going to die for is a little less controllable.

Out of all the different scenarios, my choice seemed the most concrete. I can know what I can do and what I am going to do. I can't say the same for other people around me.

I would choose to stay in my seat because only then could I truly insure good things could come about from this tragedy.

ONE GOOD THING

English 1301.01

Professor McKeown

When I heard "you're in this for the long haul," I am sure many things were racing through my head, the main one being "oh shit." And a few more vengeful, bitter, and angry ones. I could already tell that my plans for the next year or two were going to be altered quite a bit. When I started this escapade I guessed that was going to be hard on me and that my life was going to be anything but what I would have liked for it to be. But what can I say? "Shit happens."

I stumbled upon literature on reform schools nationwide. I was anything but pleased. I decided to call my dad and see if he knew anything about it. "It's just an option we are looking into." I could not believe it. By definition a reform school is a correctional institution for the detention and discipline of young or first offenders. Wait, these types of places are for the trench coat mafia, gangsters, and Paris Hilton, not me.

My dad and I were "driving home to Waco from Houston at five in the morning because he had to be at work." Growing up as many others do, I always believed that parents spoke nothing but truth. To my surprise, they lie better than me. So at seven in the morning I wake up on a dirt road in Davy Crockett National Forest heading towards a Wilderness Treatment Program. When my stabbed-in-the-back sixth sense popped up, it was already game over.

I found myself hiking around in the woods with a seventy-pound makeshift backpack made with a strap and a sheet of plastic that was most likely purchased at a roofing supply store. I was with three therapists at a time and a group of delinquents like myself. We hiked five miles a day and took one fifteen-minute shower a week. Logistics also left out deodorant, more than two pair of socks, or any good food.

My dog that I have had since I was four died the day after. I was told they were just presoaking me in the situation that I had coming my way. Yes, reform school here I come. My month of being a rugged individual, thank God, came to a stop with a candy bar and a few necessary toiletries that I never knew could be so wonderful.

We stayed in a hotel room overnight in Houston on our route to Prineville, Oregon, a city in which a child car seat, a few scattered plastic flamingos and the family dog chained to an old transmission were common place in one's front yard. I was on my way to a compound of small dorms for communal living with cough-drop snorting, meds-checking, and gasoline huffers thirty miles into the Ochoco National Forest.

I walked in admissions and asked about the overall policies of the place. All the important things I was hoping to be available were not. Well by the time my shaky optimism is snuffed completely, I was taken away to be strip-searched and inventoried.

I was engulfed in a violent windstorm of therapy, yelling, and readily available personnel to be professional pessimists toward every aspect of my life. This is where I started a year that can be summarized quite quickly because of the repetitive nature of the place. Monday through Thursday we cleaned, went to school, ate and slept. On Tuesday and Thursdays we had group therapy from two to five. Plus any other matters that needed an all school group that normally lasted around eight hours. On Friday we played sports sometimes. On Saturdays we cleaned all day the watched a PG 13 film with some therapeutic relevance such as Patch Adams or Radio, and got an off brand soda at dinner.

I had an emotional breakdown and was hospitalized in a lockdown in San Marcos. My dad told me I could leave when I finished high school, thinking I could not until my release date which is many months away still. Well I am seventeen and in college because someone told me I could not.

Bad things happen but even throughout these you can find at least one thing that was worth something personally meaningful. I graduated two years of high school in nine months. I am back home with most of my friends and family. Enjoying life. And most important of all, the knowledge that I have been institutionalized enough to disqualify me from any military draft that G.W. Bush might create if he rigs the vote again.

MARIJUANA

There are many views about marijuana and why it should or should not be legal; unfortunately most of these are negative and made by people who are not well informed. I think if more people were informed about the negative effects of its criminalization then there would be more thinking before making a decision about whether or not a dying AIDS victim is a criminal that deserves to be in federal prison with murderers and rapists because smoking marijuana eases their pain. It's funny how things work out in America.

I think one of the facts that more people should know about is that a lot of people are making money off marijuana being illegal. Mjlegal.org reports that some of these are paper, drug, medical, alcohol, tobacco and prison industries, not to mention government drug sales to finance foreign wars. Mpp.org states that tremendous amounts of money are made by prison officials. It is not unusual for guards and other officials to sell marijuana to the inmates that are there because of dealing in the first place. "Rape of Incarcerated Americans: A statistical look" states that victims are more likely to be young, small, non-violent, first offenders and middle class. I think that fits quite too many people that get arrested for possession. Another way of seeing how the prison system and government make money off of marijuana users is that the more people that can be incarcerated, the more money they can make from dealing drugs to them and using them for labor. People should also see that if we legalize marijuana it will make the government money because due to legalization many states will be able to grow marijuana as a cash crop, and the U.S. government will be able to tax marijuana and make revenue off of it.

This is also something that never made much of any sense to me, the government gets to confiscate all possessions from anyone arrested for marijuana. You can murder someone and go to jail for the rest of your life and still get to keep your property even if just to your kids, but get caught with one joint or a field full and you own nothing.

Smoking marijuana is not an inherently criminal activity. I think there is a big difference between doing something illegal and being a criminal. I think there is a difference between Rosa Parks and Charles Manson. They both did something illegal but I only think one was a criminal.

Many respectable people in the medical profession know that marijuana has very positive effects on its users for medical uses. The American Medical Association concluded that marijuana is one of the safest therapeutic active substances known. No one has ever died from an overdose, and it has a wide variety of therapeutic application. The Virginia Nurses

Association (VNA) concluded that these include relief from nausea and increase of appetite, reduction of intraocular pressure, reduction of muscle spasms, and relief from chronic pain. These are some of the conditions that can reap the rewards of the legalization of medical marijuana: AIDS, cancer, multiple sclerosis, epilepsy, and chronic pain as well as depression and other disabling mood disorders.

There are numerous organizations that have recently taken positions in support of legal access to medical marijuana and/or opposing the criminalization of medical marijuana using patients, including AIDS Action Council, American Academy of Family Physicians, American Bar Association, American Public Health Association, California Medical Association, California Legislative Council for Older Americans, California Pharmacists Association, California Society of Addiction Medicine, Consumer Reports magazine, Lymphoma Foundation of America, Multiple Sclerosis California Action Network, National Association of People With AIDS, the New England Journal of Medicine, and the American Medical Association. It's hard to believe that even with all those positive, credible resources that realize that medical marijuana could be a very positive and efficient medical option that still the government still keeps it away from people who have cancer.

I have had a close friend who had cancer and went through chemotherapy. That just leaves me wondering how medical marijuana could have helped him. He had to deal with sticking a two-inch needle into his stomach every day, I want to know if some of the politicians had to deal with that, how they would stand on the issue.

Consider the billions of dollars that are spent on keeping marijuana users in jail and the war on drugs going in circles. Now think about how AIDS studies in Africa could be funded or how starving children in America could use some food, or maybe how that could go to public inner city schools that are worn down and out of date. The war on drugs is just like any other war; it's going to be ugly and leave scars, it's going to kill and ruin innocent people, and it is most likely to produce profit for the group who waged it.

Sources

mjlegal.org

jou.ufl.edu

"Marijuana as Medicine: a plea for reconsideration," The Journal of American Medical Association: June 21, 1995.

Stephen Donaldson, "Rape of Incarcerated Americans: A preliminary look," Stop Prisoner Rape, New York, NY: 1995.

Henry Hyde, "Forfeiting Our Property rights: is your property safe from seizure?" Washington D.C. Cato Institute, 1995.

CRIMINALIZE IT

English 1301_34
Professor McKeown

All societies have to deal with issues of drugs and other intoxicants. What generally occurs is problems caused by users have to be dealt with by others affected. In my research I have found some examples of these problems in three arenas of life. These are the driving and motor skills, workplace, and social interactions.

The first and main reason I believe that marijuana can pose a problem is that it affects its users' ability to drive. Driving while intoxicated on any substance is dangerous. We already know how many alcohol-related accidents occur each year, and another easily available drug would have a greater chance of falling to an irresponsible user's hands and they could pose problems on the road. Most marijuana users drive below the speed limit; this is a problem just as speeding is. While alcohol has a much stronger effect on motor skills, marijuana still limits a driver's abilities. Marijuana also impairs a person's internal measure of time. This could create a problem in their driving if they are trying to rush somewhere. Short-term memory is jeopardized while intoxicated; this can lead to confusion while driving.

Another area that I find to be limited by use of marijuana is in the workplace. Because of its obvious toll on the memory it could be detrimental to professions that require this function, such as waiters and waitresses. I say this because they have to take orders, and having to come back to the same table three times to ask what type of soda they wanted isn't going to help that person excel. Another way that marijuana can negatively affect a professional life is that users have a higher chance of being late or absent to their professional obligations because of the lack of a proper grasp of time.

Also I have noticed that marijuana can make a difference in someone's social interactions. Since marijuana is illegal, it is bought and sold on the black market. Many times these drug dealers sell more than just marijuana and this can introduce many people to be introduced into harder drugs. Smoking anything causes health issues such as asthma, chronic bronchitis, and emphysema. Just as passive smoke from cigarettes will cause respiratory problems in nonsmokers, the same rule applies here. If there is a nonsmoker in a room full of people smoking, they too have to consume smoke.

Right now America is the fattest nation in the world. I say this because of the fact that marijuana stimulates the appetite. If it was as available as alcohol, it would further the epidemic of obesity.

These are the main reasons I think marijuana should not be available to the general public. I have looked into different sources so that I would have a more vast understanding of the topic. There is a saying that the worst thing about Christianity is Christians. The worst thing about any intoxicant is an irresponsible user.

MARIJUANA: MISUNDERSTOOD

English 1301_34
Professor McKeown

"There are 100,000 total marijuana smokers in the U.S., and most are Negros, Hispanics, Filipinos, and entertainers. Their Satanic music, jazz, and swing, result from marijuana use. This marijuana causes white women to seek sexual relations with Negros, entertainers, and any others." This is what America's first drug czar, Harry J. Anslinger had to say about marijuana in 1937.

He proposed the first Congressional action that led to the lasting criminalization that we still have to live with and pay for today. He argued that "marijuana is an addictive drug which produces in its users insanity, criminality, and death," as well as, "marijuana is the most violence-causing drug in the history of mankind." I am thinking that the argument that sealed the deal back in good old 1937 was that "marijuana makes darkies think they're as good as white men." (Peter Guither)

I am hoping that most Americans would know that these kind of racist, immoral, and unscientifically based reasons would not hold up in Congress today, but what they probably do not know is that they held up back then and those laws that we set forth

67 years ago still govern the direction of our judicial system. I believe that marijuana laws as we have now hold more harm than benefits for Americans. What I believe should happen is that marijuana should be listed in the same category as alcohol and tobacco.

I do not believe that marijuana is harmless. I believe that it should be governmentally regulated, taxed, and controlled. Here are the reasons for my opinion, the first being that there has not once been a death from marijuana in the history of mankind. Tobacco is the number one preventable cause of death in the United States, and alcohol overdoses and accidents stay ranging in huge numbers.

The second reason is that it is not addictive. Alcohol and tobacco are highly addictive. There is a huge market in aids to quit smoking cigarettes as well as Alcoholics Anonymous and various other groups with the intent to help people dependent on these legal intoxicants.

The third is that inhaling the smoke of a burning plant is bad in any condition. But most smokers of marijuana smoke much less of a quantity to that of a cigarette smoker, my case being I know many people who smoke a pack a day and no one who smokes twenty joints by themselves a day.

The main reason politicians use for why we should keep marijuana illegal is the "Gateway Theory." This is completely twisted to get a propagandized view across from uninformed politicians. They try to back up their theory by saying that a large number of

cocaine users used marijuana previously. What they fail to publicize is that 83% of the Americans who have used marijuana have not used cocaine. This is a huge majority and proves that the "Gateway Theory" is just that a theory created by politicians and marijuana prohibitionists.

We have 77 million Americans in prison or in jail right now for marijuana offenses, most of which are possession charges. If you grow one marijuana plant, no matter how small, you commit a federal felony. You can grow hallucinogenic mushrooms and poppies, but until you cut, dry or process them in any form, you are free from prosecution. Also, on a different note, large cultivators of marijuana face more stringent penalties then those who commit manslaughter or auto theft. On average, the war on marijuana alone costs American taxpayers around 12 billion dollars annually.

Prohibition causes major problems in our society. I am a freedom-loving American and believe that the truth about the safest of the three top intoxicants in the United States should be known by all. By having government run propaganda against marijuana makes the truth an inconvenience to their mission, and I cannot support an idea built on lies.

I make decisions based on reason and truth, not on out-of-date immoral and scientifically nonexistent arguments made 67 years ago. As the casualties of the war on marijuana increase, I can only hope that the national conscience on this issue will increase with it.

MEMORIES LIVE ON

English 1301.01
Professor McKeown

Last April, my best friend committed suicide. The life and the death of my friend impacted every aspect of my life. I first met Taylor through stories that my partner in English class would tell me, never revealing the name out of respect and privacy for her. I could respect this but it was straining on my patience. I just wanted to meet this person. She sounded amazing: irreverent, rebellious, funny, kind, openly imperfect. It was odd to me how someone would be so honestly human. When we first met we instantly started talking like old friends, like we had grown up together and fallen out of touch. She took my life, which seemed to me at the time a finished piece, and turned it into a work in progress.

We grew closer and closer together, spending all of our free time together. We could have been in a relationship except I had a girlfriend at the time, but looking back on it I think it could have been too deep of a friendship to turn into anything else. We spent the majority of our time together on her family's property. They owned a big part of land in between Waco and Lacy Lakeview that held three small houses that her father rented out. We would go canoeing, swimming, exploring. I even watched her learn to drive stick shift on all the back roads (an unforgettable experience I must say).

As we spent more and more time together I started noticing things like how she viewed the "big picture." It would have been less important if it were less detailed. I must admit I was humbled by the generosity, compassion, and good intent of her "big picture."

I never knew someone, personally, so interested in the well-being of others. She would place the well-being of her friends above her own. Also she took interest in the well-being of the things that I pass up every day. I once walked in a dried up creek bed so I wouldn't have to stumble through the underbrush until I was bum rushed by someone yelling, "You're killing the ecosystem!" Apparently being trampled on stunts the fragile growth and sustainability of the future inhabitants of this creek bed. I believe that an action of putting yourself and comfort level behind the well-being of microorganisms in a dried up creek bed is more compassion that I have ever seen in a person.

Ironically this mentality of putting others before herself would be one of her greatest flaws. People could easily lead her into jeopardizing her own beliefs. She was never a follower yet she could easily be led. She was also gullible. Too trusting. She had such a good view of the world that she was unaffiliated with the manipulative, the greedy, and the "I'm gonna get mine" mentality; unfortunately for her others knew and lived these ways around her. She often found herself preyed on because of this.

Because of this atmosphere that she produced with all of this trusting compassion, I became completely open. I have never trusted someone the way I trusted her. There is something that we experience as people when we know someone "has the dirt on us" that leaves us feeling unguarded. The thing about her is that she could have known anything and everything and I would feel as if she was part of my shield.

I loved how irreverent she could be. I think that there is no freedom in watching out for what might potentially ruffle someone's feathers the wrong way. That was something I never saw her do. She was herself and if someone did not like it, so what. It was rare in a high school setting to find too many girls with this kind of attitude. I loved it.

I was in reform school when I was called into the director's office to receive a phone call telling me that Taylor had died. I could not believe what I heard. At the time I was unaware of what pure sorrow and grief felt like. I soon became well acquainted with the two. The experience made me think about how important each moment of intentional goodness is. How every second you spend with people you love can outweigh the countless hours in front of a TV or commuting. I came back to Waco in August. Now I am trying to live in a way that would make Taylor say, "Hell yes."

With Taylor Mosley.

With Taylor Mosley.

MY EXPERIENCES WITH WRITING

English 1301.01
Professor McKeown

My experiences with writing have been in a large way a release. My mind cannot keep up with the rest of me so when I write it makes it possible to put what I'm thinking down on paper. This is how I started writing.

The first time I wrote for fun I was having a difficult time in my life and I started writing poetry. It was all a bunch of mopey, 13 year old, stale stuff, but you have to start somewhere. My writing skills improved and my writing styles became more eclectic. Now in my writing I use metaphors to get to something deeper. I think people have better chances conceiving the big picture if you put it in bite-sized fashion. People are more likely to eat the hors d'oeuvres before the feast.

I started writing on my own but two people stick out in my mind as those who influenced me the most. These were my good friend Brittle and my English teacher Elizabeth White.

Brittle was an inspiration more than a teacher. We were extremely close so it drove me to write. Most of it was a little different subject matter than the first stuff I got started on.

My English teacher and I were more like friends. I knew her in middle school. We would go off to a coffee shop during school hours. She taught a writing class but I didn't go. We hung out and watched independent movies and went and had fun together. We went to an abandoned slaughter house and dressed up in costumes at Wal-Mart at 3 in the morning. She did more short stories than I did and that opened my mind's eye onto that scene. I used to keep writing journals with stories and poetry but people not of my choosing went prying. That happened a few times and I quit writing for a while. I still don't write too much.

When I was at a treatment center in San Marcos I wrote a nine-page short story about a bird who stretched his wings too much and so its parents sent him straight down to the moles below their nest that looked as though they had their life together. It's the story of a bird who is a failure as a mole and once he tries to be a bird again his wings won't work anymore because the moles taught him that moles don't use wings.

The story ends with him stretching his wings to fly over a pond. Needless to say, he sinks. It was a huge metaphor for the chain of events that I had been going through.

I write to have a release. I don't naturally edit the vocal content that I give off so I have to do the composure on paper. I write best when I'm alone. I get distracted easily so I usually listen to music. One of my weaknesses in writing are that when I get into a style that only lasts for a short period of time. So when I really like how I'm writing I write a lot. I think that writing is more powerful than speech alone because it materializes your thought process.

Most of what I read as I got started was my friend's poetry and mopey song lyrics. Some of the authors that inspired me are George Orwell, Irvine Welsh, Shel Silverstein and a little more soulful artists.

When I write, I don't read it that day and I very rarely make any changes. Overall writing is a way to collect my thoughts and feelings and place them down on paper.

POETRY, NOTES, & DRAWINGS

Alex with his nephew,
Jon David Ware, 2005 – 2009.

ENTITLEMENT

Rich men telling poor people how they

Understand poverty.

Healthy treating the sick.

Excuse me Mr. Therapist,

When was your last breakdown? Huh?

You can't understand pain until you get hurt.

Privilege breeds entitlement but so does poverty

feb 21

11:30 pm

yea yn, tonight is one of
those nights, you know the
died ????? cigarette nights.
????? to a ????? ????? ?
??? ????? believes me when
i say i am bipolar. "-tank god"
i noticed today for the first
time that i'm lonely. I have
one hand in my pocket, and
the other pocket has dope
money, cigarettes, and depilits.
i kind of miss audra. but she
did run my life for the most
part. i went to sleep so bad.
the moon is real bright tonight.
i'm writing this in moonlight.
Nothing can ever get better or
worse? I used to tell brittany
that the sole cure for
any ailment was hot tea.
well i need some fuck of tea,
and a good friend. I wish
i didn't have to fight all
my battles alone.

MADONNA BEGGED

Madonna begged
for a place to stay
from a perfect stranger
she had no money
so she wound up in a
manger
welfare mothers in
social security, being
rationed out resources
insufficiently, and over
burdened by the
weight of inequity
narcissistly indulgent
escapist mentality
gentle by nature
coping with inescapability
constantly in need
required distractibility
so I acquired ADD
sleepless, worrying about waking up the next day

---

internal clock, incongruent with the numbers,
keeping me awake
will powerless to the anxiety
my mind tends to create
sleep deprivation is no excuse
for the well rested
she's privately voyeuristic
inherently full of sin
preconceptually speaking
where oh where to begin
her looks can be misleading
if you're reading what she writes
she lies between the
lines, fixing light of
insight.
her poise is dishonest
her moral standing weak
she powders her nose
both inside and out
never reaping what she
seeks. by cultivating the
seed of doubt
she's quick to quote the scripture

if it aids in her defense

privately voyeuristic, invisibly courageous

false belief that our idols and deities will

come down here and save us

i am my own adversary

and my only true friends

in a "heuristic" of oppression

we pretentiously defend

sink or swim, fight or flight

i'll be alright, if I make it

through the night

out of sight, from the watchful

blind

originally sinful, we ate

from the tree

the protest of human nature

we call morality

continue into incoherency

exhausting, never to be read

promotion of pointlessness

barely making sense

basically wasting paper and ink

Original Sin

you gotta start somewhere...

The original sin that delivered
the fall of mankind was
the persuit of wisdom
from the forbidin tree
bearing the fruit of
knowledge.

CHAOS

Why are we instigating
coups in the oil rich Middle east
When theres babies with HIV
in Africa that need something to
eat.

No potable water for anyone
to drink, season pass to
schliterbaun, what will make you
think.

the starving get the scraps
off the plates of the obese.

Sense when has senseless
violence, been the path
twords civil peace?

Animosity from the weathy
to the the people in the streets
to damning welfare mothers for
finding food to eat.

Why do we blindy trust
a system of deciept?
that Everyone knows is made
to benifet the elite.

counterfit wisdom creating
the illusion of freedom
confusion consumes them

The empty
pursuit
of
Every Tree
Bearing the
Wrong
fruit.

Eve Was So

Naieve

Soulful observation
decays ~~the~~ ability see
handicaped perseption·
the truth shall set you free

Objective observation is
the nature of reality

conflicting motius
propell us) to be free~~doms~~

~~who~~ watching, who cares,
it look like, is it ~~fair?~~ fair?

is it just, or just because?

all it does is what it does.

we all fall down ~~when~~ we fall in love.

He's ~~always~~ falling down, no matter how
hard he tries.

Because all he wants is truth
in a matrix of lies.

He's begging for god getting
lord of the flies.

lais é fair gratification
as long as I get mine
passifyed restlessness
leaving you behind
getting over on others
just to meet the needs
of a needy, fickle, mind
Getting ahead in this world
requires leaving some behind.
the strong survive, by pairing
up with weakness.
aplication to a creed of violence
breeds ~~recklessness~~ in persuit of
recklessness
get away with unpardonable deeds
following a creed of scilence

WHY DO WE WASTE
SO MUCH TIME?

Love is all that matters

Everything else is pretend.

Find your center

And share joy.

Pass on empathy

And hug a stranger.

Everything is connected.

God's love is not reserved

For Christians or mankind.

Love is infinite

And love is blind.

All the pandas and centipedes

Share the immense love of their creator.

Emancipate yourself from suffering.

Heal yourself from the inside out.

Mend your wings and believe in freedom.

Appreciate every moment you have.

It's the fucking small things.

As I was sitting in my father's Mercedes Benz

Listening to explicit rap music at full banging volume

I looked over into the next car and saw an old woman

I smiled at her and she to my surprise smiled back.

For a second I made a connection

Smile at everyone you can get to make eye contact.

PARADOX

The mind is a paradox
Of limitless possibilities
And options.
Right and wrong
Look at what is there
The majority of
People's collective thought
Is based in how closely
You can categorize
Interpret and understand

sitting duck
poised on the ripples
ignoring its reflection
floating on the waters
perfect receptive

aquatic intuition

~~ccrior of~~

~~the~~ vally of jog hill
I sit on a
misrepresentation I overlook
trasspassed to the greater view

ve pray for peace
thirst ~~for~~ hope
vibrate with love
paint with compassion

please deliver us all.

QUANDARY

Put the fluffball of a spoiled cat in the Fancy Feast commercials in the forest and watch. It will be completely defenseless. It will have a grenade but not know how to use it. If you can't use it, it's useless. We wouldn't do this to a house cat. We turned a natural being of the universe and transfered our perversions on nature onto it. Get survival on a silver platter and get it a Gucci sweater and Louis Vuitton carrying case.

.

Mind your Mind

NEVERMIND

Your

MIND

when
you

Find your Mind

Bind your Mind

Play tricks on
minds
that
Play tricks on
Us

contemplate
to
chew
masticate with thought
seek to
understanding
to
map it out
to
figure it out
to
put pieces together
to
puzzle to puzzles
to
sunthisize into thought

LIQUOR STORE INCENSE

I am aware

Happiness smells

Like liquor store

Incense.

This pretense is

too intense to

transcend and converse

to love

enjoi e"N-JOY"

BE MORE AWARE

Practice on strangers. How to be more compassionate to people we don't know. Like all things it is how we process other people, perception is reality. If we see an angry person we should not be angry back. We should hope that something good happens so that person may be happier.

Pray for the people in the ambulance that many of us just see as another excuse to slow the driving progress to work. Put yourself in other people's shoes. There are poor people in the world who would do anything for a handful of water just to keep from dehydration or getting dysentery from the water and we go to waterparks.

Think outside yourself. Cry because your friend's grandmother dies. Suffer when others are in pain and what better act of empathy to be empathetic is to grasp, not imagine how that must feel. Don't judge anything as what you find it to be, because the projected image is only a painting of a face on a burka in Pakistan.

Find the soft spot, our humanness, our oneness that the whole world possesses. When you think of a ghetto, thug, drug dealer, don't see the addiction feeding and violent capitalism. Be open to seeing him sing the ABCs to a 3 year old girl who knows this thief, gangster, hoodlum as one thing . . . Daddy.

if we repeat ~~the~~ our wrongs
we seal our fate

wanting to belong, we
misplace our hate

~~~~ colored folks are
still irate, shackles to
handcuffs, nothings changed,
chain-ganged Kunta-Kintes,
still property of the state.

Andy Grifith & Barny Fife
had a tune they'd sing,
nowadays cops can
get away with anything
Brutely justifing the
death of rodny king.

fufill the expectation of
playing the steriotypes

dance a jig you ~~silly~~
jigaboo bring smiles to ~~the~~
whites

Blessings from the corrupt
Santifing the spiritualy amuck,

Pilgrem to meca, You go to babylon
self-ritiously ~~propaga dulcing~~
giving merit ~~to the holness~~
of all your wrongs.

judicial system further
insuring ~~that~~ the minority to
fail
they imprison the poor
knowing they can't post
bail.

patiently aweting, ~~Betated~~
~~justice~~, courtdoke's months
away, he has a court
~~apointed~~ lawler never seen his
face,

~~got~~ his peers found no
~~cause~~ to deliberate
~~the~~ thought he'd find justice
they just put him in his place

one ~~more~~ more innocent ~~they~~
man they incarcarate.

driven mad by injustice, silenced
by rape, preocupied by the threat
of every cell mate. This was
wrong, property of state, shot to
death running twords justice, tring
~~to~~ escape

LAISSEZ-FAIRE SURVIVALISM

Self emancipation from
Inconsistent expectations
Prerequired exploitations
Insuring the
Overpowering and subjection of the weak.
Moral secession from
A moral lesson,
Editing integrity to fit
Your needs
Making makeshift morality more convenient
To the inequity it breeds
Propinquity is the casualty
Of self-servitude.
Being the best
Ain't easy.
With a restless mind
Idle hands and a
Trifling soul.
Praying every day, for God to
Make us whole.

PROTECT AND SERVE

Blind judgment feels out kinky hair

Protecting and serving Babylon

Federally funded terrorists

With Absolute Authority

Something to prove with

A badge and nine

All making sure they

Make their quota on time.

Aiming their loaded pistols

Toward the impoverished

Minority.

Morality, unconstitutionally

A self regulated

Ethically degenerated,

Ethnically intimidated,

Constitutionally bankrupt,

Billy clubbed and silenced

They uphold civil peace

By unrivaled violence.

Intimidation, deception, and a reliance on

Public ignorance to
Carry out judiciously
Sinister agenda,
Our protectors
Habitually, intentionally
Violate our
Unalienable rights
Bastardizing the
Moral code that you
Were meant to uphold.
Brutalizing the public
You were paid to protect,
You mace out the eyes
Of the patriots you
Victimize.
Victimless crimes
Turning the
Peaceful into criminals.
Privatized, corporate,
State run, slave plantations,
A junior college
Career plan, put my
Personal liberty in your

Hands
You have socially
Acceptable shackles
Itching at your waist
Right next to you
Taser, Billy club, mace
Nullifying the legal
Foundation put forth
By our forefathers
So you can jeopardize
The liberty in which
We all pursue.
You thrive in a hostile
Fire ant like support
I am exhausted by
This misuse and abuse of
Power.
An "unbiased"
Application of force.

I'M THE SHIT WITH
A GUN AND A BADGE

I'm the shit with a gun and a badge, here to protect

and to serve our rights,

taught how to keep them far away, let me search

you, call the K-9, call my

parents, call my lawyer. I'm the shit with a badge

and a gun, go from taking a bite

out of crime to a life out of a nigger. Love it dare to

resist drugs and violence.

Protect my rights? Is that the job description? Missed

the memo. Everything I

learned about you in kindergarten you're the one

to call. A cop protecting and

service my rights is about as likely as Jerry Falwell

conducting a gay marriage.

Scruffy the crime dog to Rodney King, We're angry

because we know the truth.

WAR ON DRUGS

Our culture is obese and our icons are anorexic. Diet pills are filled with a drug that keeps narcoleptics awake and children's eyes on the chalkboard and feet on the ground.

Our lifestyles are so incredibly fast paced that we have reached beyond our limitations. Some people have to supplement with pills that would have truckers working for days on end.

This is a good example of drugs of abuse progression with the war on drugs. Social tolerance. Epidemics have on a timeline moved from marijuana to methamphetamine.

It's what the gateway theory looks like in my head. We went from smoking plants to smoking chemicals. Are we winning the war?

The war on drugs is really a war on counter cultures and people of color.

Marijuana – Hispanics, Blacks, Jazz

LSD – the anti-war movement, hippies, beatniks, activists

Crack – Blacks, poor people

Ecstasy – modern day hippies called ravers with less politics and more love. Creed is Peace Love Unity Respect

Methamphetamines – rural whites, bikers, Sudafed

Fortunately the theory of gateway drug has been scientifically and statistically proven wrong, while more and more scientific studies continue proving its extremely safe nature to both medicinal and recreational users.

In 2002 45.3% of total drug arrests were for marijuana. 620,541 of these for possession alone.

Alcohol and tobacco are both legal, accepted, and widely taken part in. They are both physiologic and psychologically addictive, harmful to your health, and both rank in the top three causes of death in the US. Neither one has any medical use except to disinfect open wounds.

Marijuana is not addictive on any level nor has it killed even one person. It has a wide range of medical uses and the intoxication doesn't impair coordination like alcohol. Impaired driving on alcohol, swerving speeding recklessness. Marijuana – slowed reaction time, driving slower.

Gateway theory of my own. There is a need in our animal nature, a need for altered states of mind. When you see a child spinning to become dizzy, they are being introduced to this.

Our laws still suffer from reefer madness and the fact that Phillip Morris stuffs funds into politician's pockets, assuring the triumph of brand name cancer addiction.

Marijuana – legalize it. Remember prohibition? The mob was powerful and wealthy because of alcohol prohibition.

Today there is an epidemic of methamphetamines, most likely due to the ecstasy epidemic and the war on raves in the late 90s where PLUR met SWAT. Also, giving three-year-olds medical amphetamines because they're hyper set us up.

NO BLACK PRESIDENT?

Most prevalent source of accepted racism in the country.

In 1986, before mandatory minimums for crack offenses became effective, the average federal drug offense sentence was 11% higher than whites. Four years later it was 40%.

The majority of crack offenses involve blacks; white people do cocaine. Crack is cocaine and baking soda. The process usually triples the amount but not the amount of the only active ingredient – cocaine.

Crack sentences vs. cocaine are much more severe. Nationwide 1 in 20 black men over 18 are in prison compared to 1 in 180 white men.

The voting population of black men is 10.4 million. 1.46 million of that population can't vote because of felony convictions.

Now it's political. No black president, why? He's in jail with the rest of the brothers.

RANDOM OBSERVATIONS OF LIFE

- Marbles – I'm not sweatin' them lost marbles. What was I going to do with them anyway? Play marbles?

- If you misspell but know you do are you more or less able?

- Do we learn more from reading, memorizing and spelling the sentence?

- The chicken or the egg or from thinking about what came first?

- On spiritual guides / teachers – they introduce the information in which the student teaches themselves with.

- Antidisestablishmentarianism – the biggest words are spelled how they sound.

- Culture without TV mainly would be an extremely big step in the direction of our society but an impossible act to be done by the government because it would jeopardize many constitutional freedoms.

- Does it matter if you're a genius if you can't write or talk?

- Education doesn't matter if you can't be graded. If grades didn't matter more people would learn.

- If you think intelligent thoughts and forgot them? Can you unthink? Thinking is something that man has lost control of, been let go of, yet can direct. We can put more lines in the sand than a Caribbean Tony Montana, but regardless the high tide will come, and it doesn't matter what you do, eventually the ocean will take back and give you a whole beach to scratch up again.

- Humans have domesticated themselves. We may be eating Fancy Feast now but what happens when we run out of canned food. That will be the apocalypse. We created the idea of "the end of the world" translates into the end of humans. When we completely absolve ourselves of being connected to this world by having a manmade way of surviving.

- "We are in control." The best way to feel in control is to twist a perception of control into something we can measure and name as control. The best way to be in control is to let go of it.

- Our ability to think has made us conquer everything except nature. We may be going with the flow, but the flow is flowing, we just aren't aware.

- It's like how they lock up animals in small cages and cut off their beaks to protect the other ones because they go crazy being locked up and having their beaks cut off.

- The look of terror in the eyes of an animal being hurt, just like us. To a seal mother weeping at a beach seeing its pup being eaten by someone else. Compassion to our own species is easier when we look for similarities instead of constantly creating and twisting the differences.

- The awkward feeling we get when we are at a red light in an expensive ass car avoiding eye contact with the homeless man with a sign announcing to the world in most cases, "GOD BLESS YOU." Hobos have already been God blessed.

- When you appreciate things you are humble. When you appreciate things excessively, you become an abuser.

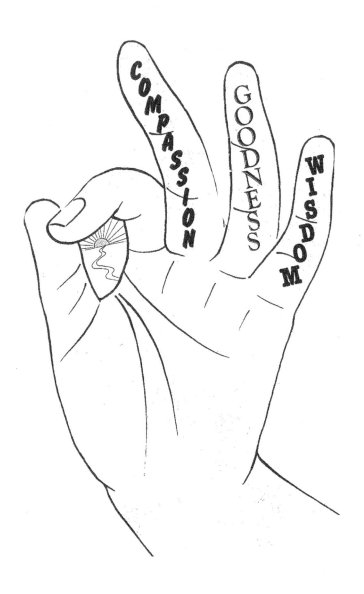

- Why help places with oil out of our love of peace, but let African children starve?

- Why isn't victimless crime an oxymoron?

- The cause of prolonged racism more violence, lower education, poor politics, narrower vision, public fear by panic endorsement.

- How it works: Man finds and utilizes fired tools thus making a ripple in the fabric of nature. We have the choice to move around in the food chain. It isn't who has the bigger teeth any longer.

- We moved from feeder rat status to having the ability to kill populations and the planet they rode in on. "Hey guys, let's try something. We are going to roshambo Mother Nature. We're going to think of a plan to kill something God did not allow us to do naturally." That's like a female sperm donor. Without moral limitations we could fuck up the natural order of things but most likely create a seed that could turn into a life.

- Starts and finishes are manmade. Cycles are natural. We are always in the middle. Balance is everything. Two extremes make mild. Everything is a paradox. We seek to understand half of it. It is or it isn't if it's both, you're crazy. You can't be happy without being sad; comparatively, you can't be sad without having happiness. You can't be rich or poor with no ATM in reach.

- Perceptions – It's better any day to be sane, controlled and controllable with only one right answer than to be crazy, liberated, and control less. Let me go because I couldn't get a grip.

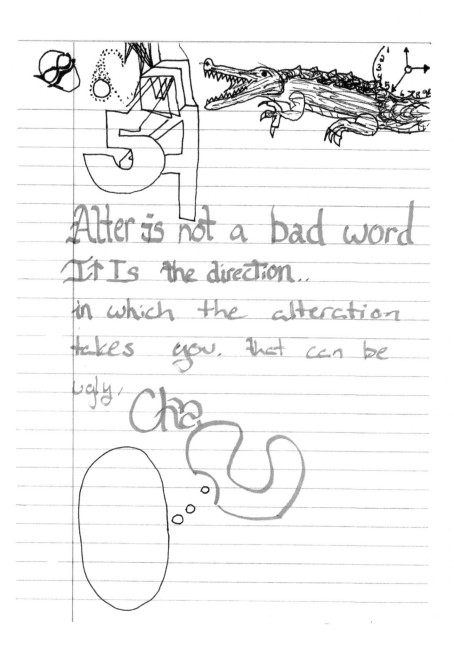

Alter is not a bad word
It Is the direction..
in which the alteration
takes you. that can be
ugly, Cha

- Sanity – Sanity can be explained as a socially acceptable way of manipulating thought. Sanity affects the mind and its ability to think, perceive, understand and ignore. If you don't have a good grip on your mind your mind could choose a multitude of options. Schizophrenics are deep thinkers because there is no limitation to the way in which they think. Sanity presents a mind with limited choice in direction.

- Use your self-awareness conscience to maintain integrity. Instead of using a roadmap, you're using a compass.

- It's like meat eaters know where meat comes from and that it is horrible. "Don't tell me that before I eat." Ignorance is bliss.

- I live this way, and so far it has proved to be challenging and difficult. You slow down systems, anger some and become outcast when you "ask questions."

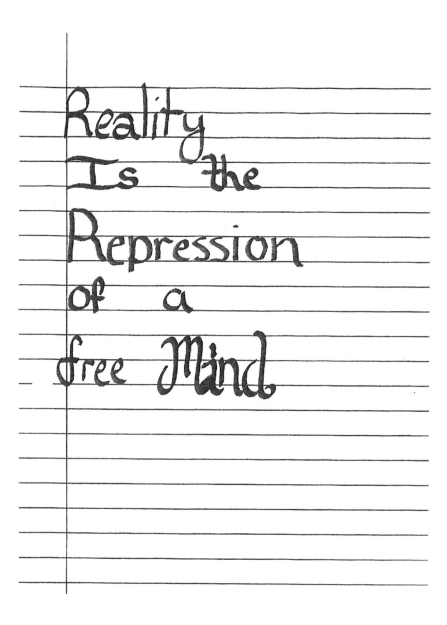

Reality
Is the
Repression
of a
free Mind

A NOTE OF ENCOURAGEMENT TO NATHAN, ALEX'S STEPDAD

October 20, 2004

Nathan,

I know you've been stressed out lately and probably sad too. Two things I do when the things happen. When something good, say it out loud "this is swell" if bad, in through the nose and out through the mouth and use the mantra "fuck it" Hold on to good stuff and let the bad stuff roll off. Things have an odd way of working themselves out . . . Keep your head up.

Love you

Alex

Alex with Nathan after a week at
Lone Star Expeditions, East Texas, 2003.

Hey,

Happy holidays, I went to my dads, came to wcco then went to San Antonio with my mother & Nathen. and right before that I went to Austin & got 2 tickets, speeding & paraphenelic. I'm going to get the p. droped because I had a drum rolled cig., with swisher tobacco. but he took my papers angery. I'll be damned, I wont pay, I'll go sit it out and they will ~~~~ hear a weekent long lecture on the injustice of marijuana laws. I got A 45 day notice here and I think im moving to the collony apts until I save enough money to go to India for a while. I got a Job at subway.

I bet I you thought,
that I you forgot,
about your mothers
day.

It mab be late
but thats okey
because
it is still today.

What I want to
say to you
is that your doing
great

And also that I
love you lots,
your the frosting
on my cake!

Happy
Mothers
Day... Love ALEX

This brings a sense of freedom from the continual whirlpool of thoughts and anxiety, of being chased by our own emotions and sensations. The ability to live in the present moment, rather than in fantasy, allows us to find delight in the world.

I was lost but now I'm found
was blind but now I see.
PLUR

pure love, only essence
sheltered forever under
the grace of god.
forgivness poured by
~~ous~~ my father, my savior
Jesus. Thank you.
Protected & surrounded
by God, Our souls finaly
~~in a blissful union~~
reunited. After all this time
what have I been waiting
for?
surrounded by the werm
hearts of dear friends
that can truely rekindle and
mend my own. I am so
blessed.

HIDE YOU

I'll hide you

I'll keep you

Warm, comfort

And protect you.

I'll hide you

Calm you down

Sedate you

Fears and help

Carry that load

Let me let you

Let it be

Let me hide you

CALM MY MIND

Please come and calm my mind. You know that you mend me. Please love me even when I don't make sense or I'm not all myself. I know it's tough to see past these things I do. Relax. Your strength makes me better. You allow me to cope through your generous sympathy. In a void you give me hope anyway.

I miss you. Thank you for all that you do for me especially when I don't deserve it or don't know. When I'm crying all I want is to find you. You let me read your book, look over your shoulder as you fill the pages, let me borrow your eraser.

Let me cling to you show you what I'll bring to you.

LET MY LEGACY BE THIS

Let my legacy be this . . . PLUR

When you choose peace

You honor me

When you love know

I'm smiling

When you come together

I'll be there too

When you are gracious

Allow me to thank you

I CANNOT STRESS ENOUGH

I cannot stress enough on the aspiration

The *essence*

of unity

the importance, strength,

truth, enlightenment,

courage, love, beauty,

essence, love,

kindness, purity,

longing, please

please please

please please

please

please get along

please love one another

love each other,

teach peace, radiance

find the light, don't ever be afraid to

pursue love, truth, peace go for it

be next to God

find joy in the ugly

NEVER

Never stop fighting for what you believe in.

Never be afraid to express what you know.

.

Please forgive me
I'll try harder let me
be good. Look past
this portrait of I
& see what I keep
inside. I apologise.

Mom,

I love you.

your son
- Alex

Please
Be Strong.

IN MEMORIAM

≕≺

MARCH 18, 1987 – MAY 15, 2006

In Memoriam

Alex Richard Ware, artist, lover of animals, poet, writer, thinker of things outside-the-box, one who longed for unity and dreamed of peace, journeyed to the other side on Monday, May 15, 2006.

A celebration of his life will be held at 4 p.m. Thursday, May 18 at Lake Shore Baptist Church with the Rev. Dorisanne Cooper and Dr. Nathan Stone as celebrants. Please join the family for a celebration party immediately following the service at Unitarian Universalist Fellowship of Waco.

Alex was born in Waco on March 18, 1987. The family that loved him and grieve at his going include his mother and stepfather, Pat and Nathan Stone; his father and stepmother, Richard and Roxanne Ware; his aunt, Karen Berger and uncle, Steve McCasland of Homer, Alaska; brothers who grieve his loss are Jason, and wife Amy Ware, and Michael Ware of San Antonio; nieces, McKenna and K'Lee and nephew Jon David Ware will miss their Uncle Alex. Special thanks to his other "brother", Jonathan and wife Sabrina Moore.

In lieu of flowers, gifts may be made to the American Civil Liberties Union; ABC (Animal Birth Control) Clinic, 1531 Wooded Acres, Waco, TX, 76710; Planned Parenthood of Central Texas, P.O. Box 1518, Waco, TX, 76703.

A CELEBRATION OF THE LIFE OF ALEX WARE

Lake Shore Baptist Church
Reverend Dorisanne Cooper

OPENING WORDS AND PRAYER

God is our refuge and strength, a very present help in trouble. Therefore we will not fear, though the earth should change, though the mountains shake in the heart of the sea; though its waters roar and foam, though the mountains tremble with its tumult. The Lord of hosts is with us. The God of Jacob is our refuge.

We are gathered here today with the strengthening fellowship of family and friends to thank God for the life of Alex Richard Ware. We are gathered as Alex's family, as his friends, as those who loved him and who love his family.

It's hard to imagine a more difficult moment than the one we now share, sitting here together at this edge of human understanding, attempting to find answers, attempting to find the right questions in the silence of someone who was precious to us and who is gone. We are altered somehow by what has happened, changed in ways we have yet to understand. Alex's sudden death has left us reeling and grief-stricken, and our loss is beyond words. His death came too early, too quickly.

And so we gather with our memories both good and difficult, with our pain, with our anger, with our questions and our overwhelming grief. But we are also gathered in gratitude for Alex's life, and the ways in which he touched various ones here. We even use the word "celebrate" today not to make light of this day or to pretend that it is not profoundly difficult, but to say that we take his life seriously in all its variations. And so, in the midst of our grief, we will hear some songs of special significance, some of which Alex had written about in his journals, one of which was already chosen for this service when yesterday Pat played this music box which hung over Alex's crib as a baby. She had not remembered that it plays "Over the Rainbow," a song with even more significance now.

It is our privilege this day to have this service in this building, for this is a place where Alex spent many of his early growing up years. Alex's Children's Minister Sharlande Sledge says "from the time he was in the church nursery and Children's Center, Alex was a whirlwind of energy and life in motion. He never wanted to miss anything—riding in the bike-a-thon, running through sprinklers on the front lawn with his friends, eating at the Children's Center Thanksgiving Feast, picking squash and potatoes in the church garden, riding to Caritas in the van at Helping Hands, 'helping' his mom build the climbing equipment on the playground she helped design."

On our pulpit here is a patchwork parament, part of a set stitched together from pieces given by church members about ten years ago. If you look closely you'll see a small piece of white jersey knit with a thin blue stripe. It's the piece eight-year-old Alex contributed, with the words penned by Pat, "Alex Ware's favorite PJs: He's had them since he was two; they just keep getting a little shorter."

Alex's life was a patchwork of so many emotions. And we are not here to pretend that life wasn't difficult for him, that he didn't have profound struggles through which his family and so many others tried mightily to reach him. But we are also not going to pretend that the way his life ended was what should define him. For this was a young man with a brilliant mind, with a gift for writing, with a connection to the world's pain.

In many ways Alex longed for the things he often wrote about, things he could not find for himself, four in particular that come up again and again in his writing—peace, love, unity, respect. And in that spirit we honor those strivings this day.

It is our comfort that Alex is not wrestling with his pain anymore, that he has finally found peace. And yet our gratitude that he no longer hurts does not make it okay with us that he is gone. Those are both truths of this day... As it is that God knows and feels our prayers. That God's unfailing love is with us and with Alex. That God's promises of hope can be trusted and can take our heaviest leaning as we remember with gratitude and pain Alex's life today. May God gather us up and grant us strength.

Shall we pray?

God of great compassion,

We bring you our grief this day, our loss, our tears, our heavy hearts at the death of this beloved son, brother and friend. We hold common grief and yet so many individual stories as well. It is our comfort that you meet each of us where we are with what we need. Draw near to each one here that we might find rest in your strength.

God of comfort, in these difficult days make your presence known to Alex's parents, to Pat, to Richard to Nathan, to Roxanne. In the morning hours when Pat awakens and looks to face the day, meet her there with a whisper of peace. Late at night when Richard is restless, may he have a sense of your comfort and care. Surround Nathan with light in his moments of darkness. Give Roxanne your tender care.

Shower your compassion on Alex's family—on Jason and Amy, McKenna and K'Lee, on Michael, on Karen and Steve, on Jonathan and Sabrina, and so many other family members and treasured friends. Pour out your love upon each of these now that they might find you companion in their pain. Hold them close to you that they might find strength in your care. And breathe through their lives in the coming days, weeks and years, that on hard days they might know of your love and on good days they might be strengthened for their own living.

Give each of us gathered here, family and friends alike, clear memories of good times with Alex to weave into the patchworks of our lives.

As our joy at having known Alex and our grief at losing him dance their way in and through each other, bring a spirit of strength to us all.

Grant us courage and gentleness and tenderness and peace,

Amen.

CLOSING WORDS AND BENEDICTION

Taken from a poem by Ted Loder and a Native American blessing

May God's gracious spirit which moves over the mysteries of living and dying, whose presence is present in budding leaves, in the call of wild geese, in the breaking of bread, in the light in another's eye and the deep longing which holds so many of us, go with you now. May you be aware of God's presence so that wonder works its mystery in you, so that passion and peace are released in your living, so that your confidence is renewed, so that you might share laughter and exchange mercy, be at ease in your struggles, bold in your loving, brave in facing down your terror, hopeful in the rising music of Christ's love in the world, joyful and grace-filled in your living.

May the footprints we each make show that we've walked in kindness toward the earth and every living thing. May our lives be a dance and may the wind broadcast peace for all generations to come.

.

ON THE FIRST ANNIVERSARY OF ALEX'S DEATH

ALEX WARE

On March 18, 1987, Alex came into our lives. On May 15, 2006, he moved from this world to the next. He left enormous holes in many hearts but also a rich legacy of generosity, compassion, creativity, and courage. Alex was a poet and made insightful observations about life.

Love is all that matters. Everything else is pretend

Why do waste so much Time?

Hug a stranger.

Everything is connected.

Heal yourself from the inside out.

Mend your wings and believe in freedom.

Misspell and write sloppy.

Be humble.

Look at eyesores.

Appreciate every moment you have.

It's the (expletive) small things.

I have faith in mankind.

Study what you have and see those who don't.

God's love is not reserved for Christians or mankind.

We came from love and it is into the comforting arms of love that we shall once again be embraced.

As I was sitting in my father's Mercedes Benz listening to explicit rap music at full banging volume I looked over into the next car and saw an old woman. I smiled at her. She, to my surprise smiled back. And it was warm and human. For a second I made a connection. Smile at every one you can get to make eye contact.

When you choose peace, you honor me.

When you love, know I'm smiling.

When you come together, I'll be there too.

– Alex

He will be remembered forever

Pat with Alex at Mount Bachelor.

You can cry because Alex is gone

Or you can smile because he lived.

Do what he wanted.

Be strong, open your heart,

Smile and go on.

– Pat Stone

POETS ARE NEVER LOST

Poets are never lost.

Not to life or the splintering thereafter

They rest between the syllables of words.

Inside the neatly tucked crevices of all the things

We wished we said and the things we wish we didn't.

They live on in the rhyme and in the rhythm

Of the way that words fall from our lips even when
they quiver.

Every sunset

Every beautiful extravaganza of life that every

Person witnesses and gives voice to holds inside it

On The First Anniversary Of Alex's Death

The voice and essence of every poet – across every lifetime.

They are never lost.

They may wander and they may wonder where to.

But the where to is an infinite.

You can find them in the trails of words they leave behind

And in the way those words settle and nest inside your heart.

– Sarah Moran, on March 18, 2015,
Alex's 28th birthday

SOME LIVES

Some lives are epics,

Some are short stories

Some are poems.

Each life has its own beauty

And its own value

And those who know that beauty

And value can enjoy it always

– Bob Flynn, written in memory of Alex

AFTERWORD

BY JASON WARE
Alex's "Bubba"

Jason, 16 years old, with Alex, 2 years old.

When I think of Alex, it is hard to limit myself to a memory or two. Alex was an extremely complex individual, and different phase of Alex's life stir up different emotions.

When I found out I was going to be a big brother, I was so excited. I was thirteen and had never been one of those before. I always thought it was so cool to be his Bubba. I enjoyed playing with him and being there as he was transforming from a baby to a little boy.

Alex visiting Jason at his job
in the shoe department at Goldstein-Migel.

After graduating high school, I enlisted in the Marine Corps. Although I was ready for this new phase in my life, I was sad to leave Alex behind. He was six and I knew that I was not going to see him very often over the next four years. I was going to miss my Little Buddy. I returned from active duty in the summer of 1995 when Alex was 11. Over the years we had lost our closeness, and shortly after I got back to Waco, Alex moved to Hereford.

The next few years of Alex's life brought about confusion. Alex struggled with who he was, who he wanted to be, and who others wanted him to be. Alex and those who loved him lived in constant confusion.

His high school years were not any better. He was spiraling out of control, and he was sent to a rehab-boarding school in Oregon. By this time, I was married and had a family of my own. I was beginning to learn just how scary it is to be a parent. I was able to visit Alex at Mt. Bachelor Academy the spring before he graduated.

I learned two valuable lessons during the week I spent with him. First, I learned, that he was not alone. There were kids from all over the country that were dealing with the same fears, failures, and issues as Alex, and there was a staff of highly trained professionals there that truly did care for him and his peers. Second, I learned that I will never be as good of a skier as Alex. I left Mt. Bachelor Academy feeling cautiously optimistic. I had seen Alex completely sober and functioning at a high level. I wanted it to always be that way.

Alex graduated and came back to Waco. Within a few months of him being home in Waco, my wife kids and I moved to San Antonio. Because of age, distance, and just being in different phase of our lives, Alex and I were never real close. We loved each other and knew that, but that was as deep as it was.

Jason and Alex at the wedding
of Pat and Nathan, May 1997.

Afterword

Jason with Alex on his 17th birthday,
Mt. Bachelor, Oregon.

I was at work when I got the call that Alex had died. Every emotion possible flooded me, but anger was the one that stuck. We all knew that this outcome was a possibility, but we never wanted to be it would happen. Two of Alex's closest friends had taken their own lives within a few years before. I was angry that Alex could be so selfish. How could he do this to his mom and dad, who loved him so much? How could he do this to me and my family? What was I going to tell my kids?

Over the years, the hurt softened, but the anger never ceased. Any time I would talk about Alex's death, I would say that he was a jerk and a coward. Those were my true feelings until August of 2014. The great actor, Robin Williams, killed himself. Why would a man who had it all take his own life at the age of 63? It was reported that he had always dealt with depression and struggled with being accepted.

I remember I prayed to God and asked him why. "God, why would Robin do this? Why would he give up? Why did he take the easy way out? Did he not leave his family? Did he not know he had a support team that would always be there for him? Why, God?"

It was not audible, but I clearly got my answer from God. God said to me, "Your brother Alex did not do what he did out of spite, anger, or hatred. He did what he did because he loved all of you very much.

He was tired of letting everyone down. He did not want his family and friends to continue on a path of setback to setback, disappointment to disappointment, and heartache to heartache. This was his way of ending all the pain one last time. This was his confused, complex way of showing his love."

As odd as this may seem and as much as this challenges my faith, I believe this to be true. So, of all of the feelings and emotions Alex has evoked people to have, I believe the greatest of these to be LOVE.

Jason with Alex.

ACKNOWLEDGEMENTS

Deepest thanks to the following:

The mountains of New Mexico and my friend Nancy Terry, who combined hard questions with gentle encouragement to convince me that Alex's words needed to be heard.

The reconnection with Alex's 7th grade Creative Writing teacher, Elizabeth White-Olson, who opened her heart and home to allow this collection of handwritten pages from a trunk to grow into a notebook.

Mark Dostert, who took Alex's writings from the stage of "only a mother would read" to a reader's tolerance.

The friends and family who both encouraged and cautioned me throughout the last six months. It was as heart-wrenching as some thought to read my son's words of pain, loneliness, and confusion. It was also enlightening to read his imaginative use of words and his observations of life.

Jason Ware, whose qualities I admire—his strength of character, even temper, and willingness to adapt to life's changes. I especially appreciate the reassuring words he wrote on a birthday card, "You're the best 'Mom' a kid could have."

Ella Hearrean Ritchie, who took this collection of memories, photos, poems, random observations, and essays and made them flow like a river.

CPSIA information can be obtained
at www.ICGtesting.com
Printed in the USA
LVOW06s0750090517
533827LV00009B/40/P